J M

Sydney's Best Picnic Spots & Beaches

GW00497110

by
Andrew Swaffer
Veechi Stuart
and Katrina O'Brien

WOODSLANE

The Sydney Morning Herald

Woodslane Press
An imprint of Woodslane Pty Ltd
Unit 7/5 Vuko Place
Warriewood NSW 2102
Australia
Email: info@woodslane.com.au
Tel: (02) 9970 5111   Fax: (02) 9970 5002   www.woodslane.com.au

First published in Australia in July 2007 by Woodslane Press

National Library of Australia Cataloguing-in-Publication data

Swaffer, Andrew.
Sydney's best picnic spots & beaches : the full colour
guide to over 100 picnic spots & beaches.

Includes index.
ISBN 9781921203152.

1. Recreation areas - New South Wales - Sydney Region -
Guidebooks. 2. Picnic grounds - New South Wales - Sydney
Region - Guidebooks. 3. Beaches - New South Wales - Sydney
Region - Guidebooks. 4. Sydney Harbour (N.S.W.) -
Description and travel - Guidebooks. 5. Sydney Region (N.S.
W.) - Description and travel - Guidebooks. I. Stuart,
Veechi. II. O'Brien, Katrina. III. Title.

919.441

Printed in Singapore by TWP
Cover photo: Hamilton Lund. Courtesy Tourism New South Wales.

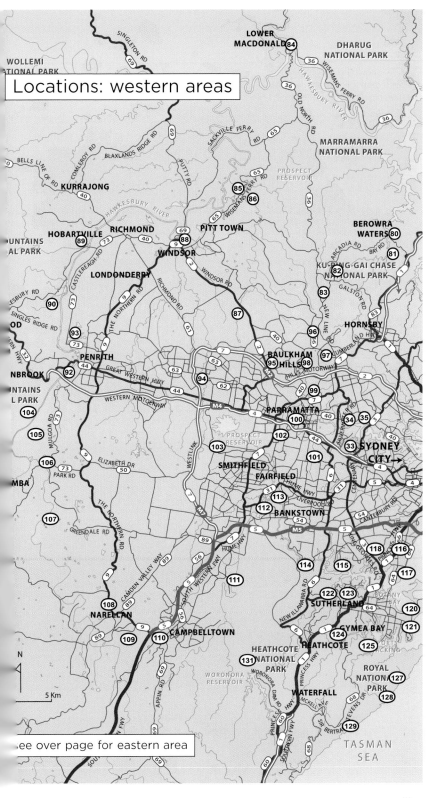

Locations: western areas

ee over page for eastern area

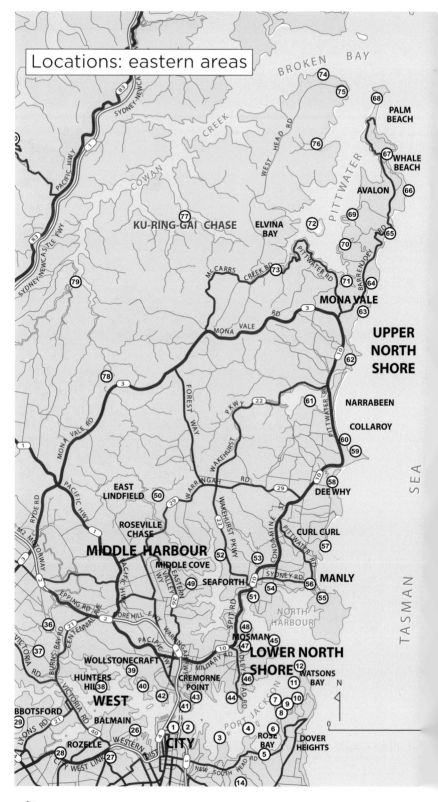

Locations: eastern areas

iv

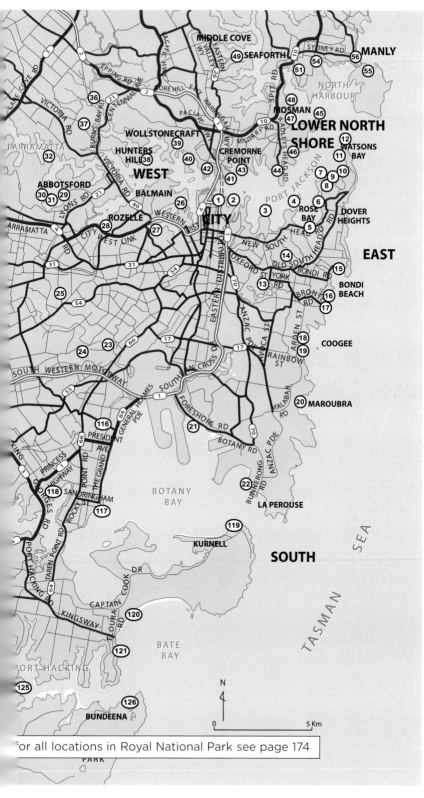

For all locations in Royal National Park see page 174

Contents

Location maps ....iii-v

About the authors 1

Acknowledgements 1

Introduction 2

    How to use this book...3

    Public transport 3

    Families and children 3

    Wheelchair access 4

    Taking your dog..4

    Looking after the environment 4

Picnic Spots & Beaches at a Glance..6

Sydney's Best Picnic Spots & Beaches

    City & Eastern Suburbs (1 to 22) 15

    Near West (23 to 38) 45

    Lower North Shore & Middle Harbour (39 to 53) 65

    Northern Beaches & Ku-ring-gai (54 to 79) 85

    North West (80 to 100)..119

    South West (101 to 115) 145

    South including Royal National Park (116 to 131) 165

Safety tips...186

Surfing Sydney's beaches...188

The 'Perfect Picnic' checklist...192

Useful addresses & contacts 193

Index 194

Other books from Woodslane and the Sydney Morning Herald........197

Photography in this book..199

Map Legend..200

About the authors

Andrew Swaffer has worked in publishing for over 15 years, several of these writing for the Footprint series of travel guides (co-authoring two Australian guides with Katrina), and now works for local Sydney publisher Woodslane. His love of the outdoors led him to develop this new series of Woodslane/Sydney Morning Herald outdoor guides.

Veechi Stuart is a freelance author, journalist and former *Sydney Morning Herald* columnist. Veechi has lived in the Blue Mountains since 1987 and is passionate about bushwalking, the local community and the environment. She is the author of two other Woodslane outdoor guides: *Blue Mountains Best Bushwalks* and *Sydney's Best Bush, Park & City Walks*.

Katrina O'Brien is a Sydney author and editor. She is co-author of the travel guides *Footprint Australia Handbook* and *Footprint West Coast Australia Handbook*, and the author of another Woodslane outdoor guide: *Sydney's Best Harbour & Coastal Walks*.

Acknowledgments

The authors would like to thank everyone at Woodslane for their encouragement and support, Coral Lee for her design and typesetting, Rebecca Robinson for the cartography, Brett Kellow (aka Surfing God) for his surfing wisdom, and Des Harris, Darroch Donald and Rebecca Robinson for many of the photographs featured in this book. For a full list of photo credits. see page 199.

Introduction

Sydney is one of the world's great cities, and frequently voted as the world's *most* enjoyable city by many global tourism bodies. The wonderful centrepiece of Circular Quay, the Opera House and Sydney Harbour Bridge has much to do with this reputation, but there's a great deal more to Sydney than these icons.

Much of the charm for residents — and for visitors with more than a handful of days to spare — is the breadth of picnic spots and beaches. There is something for everyone, from the rolling surf of Bondi Beach to the unspoilt wilderness of Ku-Ring-Gai National Park, from historic homesteads to children's adventure playgrounds. Even in a city of almost four million, there are many idyllic spots where several lazy hours can be whiled away.

The aim of the authors of *Sydney's Best Picnic Spots & Beaches* has been to try and include locations throughout the greater Sydney area, from the eastern suburbs to the base of the Blue Mountains, and from the Royal National Park to Wisemans Ferry. In doing so, we've picked out much of the very best that Sydney has to offer.

This book contains over 130 destinations, which between them offer residents and visitors a striking array of options. Most of the picnic spots are in public parks or reserves and the majority are free to ente Some are always jauntily busy, thronged with large families and grou

Cattai National Park

of friends, while others are rarely visited. Some are wonderlands for children, others are favoured by those wanting to get out and enjoy the natural surroundings for which Sydney is rightfully famous. Most of the places chosen have good facilities — tables, BBQs, toilets and playgrounds — though a few very special spots with no facilities have also been included.

How to use this book

Each destination in this book has an accompanying table giving you the basics of what to expect in the way of access and facilities. All of these destinations are summarised in a master table, starting on page 5. If you have a particular requirement — dogs must be allowed, for example — then this master table is a good starting point to quickly find out which spots or beaches are suitable. Map references refer to: G—Gregory's, S — Sydway, U — UBD.

Public transport

We have indicated public transport options, but you should always confirm service availability or times with the public transport provider before setting out. The starting points for information on most services are www.131500.info or phone 131500.

Introduction

Families and children

Virtually every destination in this book is suitable for children, and many are designed with children very much in mind. However, note that some of the coastal spots include unfenced cliff tops, exposed  lookouts or steep drops — and, of course, are near water — and adequate supervision is vital. There are a few beaches where ocean swimming, particularly for young children, is not recommended.

Wheelchair access

There are very few destinations in this book that are impossible to access with a wheelchair, and we have tried to accurately indicate ease of access. Toilet facilities are, however, much thinner on the ground, and even where access is easy, there may not be purpose-built toilet facilities.

Taking your dog

No national park admits dogs, and very few beaches allow dogs either. Otherwise you will find that dogs are allowed in most places described in this book, though usually they have to remain leashed at all times. The 'At a glance' sections will advise exactly what is possible with your dog. Taps are available at most places, and it is important to remember that your dog will want to drink just as much as you will. You'll need to clean up after your dog in any public place, so remember to go equipped with plastic bags.

Looking after the environment

You're probably already aware of the minimal impact code recommended by the National Parks and Wildlife Service: the philosophy of 'take nothing but photographs and leave nothing but footprints'. To summarise: take your rubbish with you; while walking, stay on the tracks; don't pick wildflowers or break branches; respect historical or cultural sites; and don't disturb wildlife. A copy of the code can be downloaded from the Confederation of Bushwalkers (NSW) website, www.bushwalking.org.au.

It is also important to be aware of the risk of fire. At certain times of year in the Sydney region, it only takes a single spark to create a fire that can get out of control and threaten lives and property. For this reason, total fire bans are imposed on days of extreme fire danger. Bans are issued in the afternoon and come into effect at midnight for the next 24 hours. This means that no fires of any kind may be lit in the open, but you can still use electric or gas fired barbeques provided. Some national parks may even close during total fire bans. For more information contact the NSW Rural Fire Service, T 1800 679 337, www.bushfire.nsw.gov.au.

Picnic spots & beaches at a glance

		Page	BBQs	Dogs*	Kiosk/café
City & Eastern Suburbs					
1	Royal Botanic Gardens	16	-	-	yes
2	Mrs Macquaries Point	17	-	-	-
3	Clark Island	20	-	-	-
4	Shark Island	21	-	-	-
5	Lyne Park	22	-	yes	yes
6	Strickland House	23	-	yes	-
7	Shark Beach & Nielsen Park	24	-	-	yes
8	Vaucluse Park	25	-	yes	yes
9	Parsley Bay Reserve	26	-	-	yes
10	Robertson Park	27	-	-	yes
11	Camp Cove	28	-	-	yes
12	South Head	29	-	-	-
13	Centennial Park	30	yes	yes	yes
14	Cooper Park	32	-	yes	yes
15	Bondi Beach	34	yes	yes	yes
16	Tamarama Beach	36	yes	yes	yes
17	Bronte Beach & Bronte Park	37	yes	yes	yes
18	Coogee Beach	38	yes	yes	yes
19	Grant Reserve	39	yes	yes	-
20	Maroubra Beach	40	yes	yes	yes
21	Sir Joseph Banks Park	41	yes	yes	-
22	Frenchmans Bay & Yarra Bay	42	yes	-	yes
Near West					
23	Gough Whitlam Park	46	yes	yes	-
24	Ewen Park	47	yes	yes	-
25	Peace Park	48	yes	yes	-
26	Pyrmont Point Park	49	yes	yes	-
27	Bicentennial & Jubilee Parks	50	-	yes	-
28	Leichhardt & Callan Parks	51	-	yes	yes
29	Henry Lawson Park	52	yes	yes	-
30	Bayview Park	53	yes	yes	-
31	Prince Edward Park, Cabarita	54	yes	yes	yes
32	Cabarita Park	55	yes	yes	yes
33	Bicentennial Park, Homebush	56	yes	yes	yes

Picnic spots & beaches at a glance

Playground	Shade	Swimming	Toilets	Highlights
-	lots	-	yes	gardens, scenery, things to do
-	some	yes	yes	views, things to do
-	some	-	yes	isolation, scenery, views
-	some	-	yes	isolation, scenery, views
yes	little	yes	yes	boat ramp, sports, things to do
-	some	yes	yes	gardens, scenery, views
-	some	yes	yes	beach, scenery
-	lots	-	yes	gardens, historic house, scenery
yes	some	yes	yes	beach, scenery
yes	some	yes	yes	cafés, scenery, walks
-	little	yes	yes	beach, scenery
-	little	-	-	scenery, views, walks
yes	lots	-	yes	scenery, walks, things to do
yes	lots	-	yes	isolation, scenery, walks
yes	little	yes	yes	beach, cafés, shopping, walks
yes	little	yes	yes	beach, walks
yes	some	yes	yes	beach, scenery, walks
-	little	yes	yes	beach, walks, things to do
yes	little	yes	yes	things to do
yes	little	yes	yes	beach, things to do
yes	some	-	yes	scenery, walks
yes	little	yes	yes	scenery, walks, things to do
yes	some	-	yes	scenery, sports, walks
yes	some	-	yes	scenery
yes	little	-	yes	scenery, views
yes	little	-	yes	views
yes	lots	-	yes	scenery
-	lots	yes	yes	history, scenery
yes	some	-	-	playground, scenery
yes	lots	-	yes	boat ramp, scenery
yes	some	-	yes	scenery
yes	some	yes	yes	scenery
yes	lots	-	yes	scenery, walks, things to do

Picnic spots & beaches at a glance

		Page	BBQs	Dogs*	Kiosk/café
Near West (continued)					
34	George Kendall Riverside Reserve	58	yes	yes	-
35	Meadowbank Memorial Park	59	yes	yes	-
36	Lane Cove National Park	60	yes	-	yes
37	Buffalo Creek Reserve	62	yes	yes	-
38	Clarkes Point Reserve	63	yes	yes	-
Lower North Shore & Middle Harbour					
39	Berry Island	66	-	yes	-
40	Balls Head	67	yes	yes	-
41	Bradfield Park	68	-	yes	-
42	Blues Point	70	-	yes	-
43	Cremorne Point Reserve	71	-	yes	yes
44	Ashton Park (Bradleys Head)	72	-	-	yes
45	Middle Head	74	-	-	-
46	Clifton Gardens	75	-	-	-
47	Balmoral & Edwards Beaches	76	-	yes	yes
48	Rosherville Reserve	78	-	yes	-
49	Harold Reid Reserve	79	yes	yes	-
50	Davidson Park	80	yes	-	-
51	Clontarf Reserve	81	yes	-	yes
52	Bantry Bay	82	yes	-	-
53	Manly Dam	83	yes	yes	-
Northern Beaches & Ku-Ring-Gai					
54	North Harbour Reserve & beaches	86	yes	yes	yes
55	Shelly Beach	87	yes	-	yes
56	Manly & North Steyne Beaches	88	-	yes	yes
57	Freshwater Beach	90	yes	yes	yes
58	Dee Why Beach	92	-	yes	yes
59	Fishermans Beach	93	-	yes	-
60	Collaroy Beach	94	yes	yes	yes
61	Narrabeen Lakes	95	yes	yes	yes
62	Turimetta Beach	96	-	-	-
63	Mona Vale headland	97	-	yes	-
64	Bungan Beach	98	-	-	-
65	Bilgola Beach	99	-	-	yes
66	Bangalley Head	100	-	-	-

Picnic spots & beaches at a glance

Playground	Shade	Swimming	Toilets	Highlights
yes	little	-	yes	sports facilities, isolation
yes	lots	-	yes	scenery
yes	lots	-	yes	scenery, walks, wildlife, things to do
yes	little	-	yes	scenery, walks
-	little	-	yes	scenery, views
yes	little	-	yes	scenery, walks
yes	lots	-	yes	scenery, views, walks
yes	little	yes	yes	views, things to do
yes	little	-	yes	views
yes	some	yes	yes	scenery, views, walks
-	lots	yes	yes	scenery, views, walks, things to do
-	little	yes	-	fortifications, scenery, views, walks
yes	some	yes	yes	history, scenery
yes	some	yes	yes	beach, cafés, scenery, things to do
yes	some	yes	yes	beach, scenery
-	lots	-	yes	isolation, scenery, walks
-	some	yes	yes	scenery, walks
yes	lots	yes	yes	scenery, views, walks
-	lots	-	yes	scenery, views, walks
yes	lots	yes	yes	scenery, walks, things to do
yes	some	yes	yes	scenery, views, walks
-	little	yes	yes	beach, scenery, walks
yes	some	yes	yes	beach, things to do
yes	little	yes	yes	beach, scenery
yes	little	yes	yes	beach
-	-	yes	yes	beach, scenery, walks
yes	some	yes	yes	beach
yes	lots	yes	yes	scenery, walks
-	little	yes	-	beach, scenery, isolation
-	-	-	-	scenery, views
-	-	yes	yes	beach, scenery
-	-	yes	yes	beach, scenery
-	little	-	-	scenery, views, walks

Picnic spots & beaches at a glance

		Page	BBQs	Dogs*	Kiosk/café
Northern Beaches & Ku-Ring-Gai (continued)					
67	Whale Beach	101	yes	-	yes
68	Palm Beach	102	yes	yes	yes
69	Clareville Beach	104	yes	-	-
70	Florence Park	105	-	yes	-
71	Winnererremy Bay Foreshore Reserve	106	yes	yes	yes
72	Scotland Island	107	yes	yes	-
73	McCarrs Creek	111	yes	yes	-
74	West Head	112	yes	-	-
75	Resolute Beach	113	-	-	-
76	The Basin	114	yes	-	-
77	Illawong Bay	115	yes	-	yes
78	Wildflower Gardens	116	yes	-	-
79	Bobbin Head	117	yes	-	yes
North West					
80	Berowra Waters	120	yes	yes	yes
81	Crosslands Reserve	121	yes	-	-
82	Fagan Park	122	yes	yes	-
83	Galston Recreation Reserve	124	yes	yes	-
84	Wisemans Ferry Park	125	yes	yes	yes
85	Cattai National Park	126	yes	-	-
86	Mitchell Park	127	yes	-	-
87	Rouse Hill Regional Park	128	yes	yes	-
88	Governor Phillip Park	130	yes	yes	yes
89	Navua Reserve	131	yes	yes	-
90	Yellow Rock Lookout	132	-	yes	-
91	Martins Lookout	133	-	-	-
92	Tench Reserve	134	yes	yes	-
93	Sydney International Regatta Centre	135	yes	yes	yes
94	Nurragingy Reserve	136	yes	yes	yes
95	Crestwood Reserve	137	yes	yes	-
96	Castle Hill Heritage Park	138	-	yes	-
97	Cumberland State Forest	139	yes	yes	yes
98	Bidjigal Reserve	140	yes	yes	yes
99	Lake Parramatta	141	yes	yes	yes
100	Parramatta Park	142	yes	yes	yes

Picnic spots & beaches at a glance

Playground	Shade	Swimming	Toilets	Highlights
yes	some	yes	yes	beach, scenery
yes	some	yes	yes	beach, scenery, views, walks
-	some	yes	yes	beach, views
yes	some	-	yes	scenery, isolation
yes	some	yes	yes	playground, scenery
-	-	-	-	boat trip, scenery, walks
-	lots	yes	yes	scenery
-	some	-	yes	scenery, views, walks
-	little	yes	-	beach, scenery, views, walks
-	-	-	-	scenery, walks, wildlife
-	some	yes	yes	scenery, walks
yes	some	-	yes	gardens, scenery, walks
yes	some	-	yes	scenery, walks
yes	some	yes	yes	boat ramp, scenery
yes	lots	-	yes	camping, scenery, things to do
yes	lots	-	yes	gardens, scenery, walks
yes	some	-	yes	playground, sports facilities
yes	lots	yes	yes	history, scenery
yes	lots	yes	yes	camping, history, scenery
-	lots	-	yes	isolation, scenery, walks
yes	some	-	yes	playground, historic house, walks
yes	some	-	yes	boat ramp, playground
-	lots	yes	yes	scenery, wildlife
-	some	-	-	scenery, views, wildlife
-	little	-	-	scenery, views, wildlife
yes	some	-	yes	playground, scenery, things to do
-	some	-	yes	scenery, things to do
yes	lots	-	yes	gardens, scenery
yes	lots	-	yes	scenery, sports facilities
yes	some	-	-	history, scenery
-	lots	-	yes	scenery, walks, things to do
yes	lots	-	yes	scenery, sports facilities, walks
yes	lots	yes	yes	scenery, walks
yes	lots	yes	yes	historic house, scenery, walks

Picnic spots & beaches at a glance

	Page	BBQs	Dogs*	Kiosk/caf
South West				
101 Auburn Botanic Gardens	146	yes	-	-
102 Central Gardens	147	yes	-	yes
103 Pimelea Picnic Area	148	yes	yes	-
104 Euroka	149	yes	-	-
105 The Rock Lookout	152	-	-	-
106 Blaxlands Crossing Reserve	153	yes	-	-
107 Bents Basin	154	yes	-	yes
108 Harrington Park	155	yes	yes	-
109 Mount Annan Botanic Gardens	156	yes	-	yes
110 Japanese Gardens	158	-	-	yes
111 Simmos Beach	159	yes	yes	-
112 Chipping Norton Lakes	160	yes	yes	-
113 Mirambeena Regional Park	161	yes	yes	yes
114 Georges River National Park	162	yes	-	-
115 Oatley Park (Lime Kiln Head)	163	yes	yes	-
South including Royal National Park				
116 Bicentennial Park, Rockdale	166	yes	yes	-
117 Peter Depena Reserve	167	yes	yes	yes
118 Carrs Bush Park	168	yes	yes	yes
119 Captain Cook's Landing Place	169	yes	-	-
120 Wanda Beach	170	-	yes	yes
121 Shelly Park & Beach	171	yes	yes	-
122 Jannali Reserve	172	yes	yes	-
123 Prince Edward Park, Woronora	173	-	yes	-
124 Audley Picnic Area	176	yes	-	yes
125 Warumbul Picnic Area	178	-	-	-
126 Jibbon Beach	179	-	-	yes
127 Marley Beaches	180	-	-	-
128 Wattamolla Beach	181	yes	-	yes
129 Garie Beach	182	-	-	yes
130 Other picnic spots in the Royal NP	183	yes	-	-
131 Woronora Dam	184	yes	yes	-

*Dogs - for beaches, allowed on promenade or foreshore only

Picnic spots & beaches at a glance

Playground	Shade	Swimming	Toilets	Highlights
yes	lots	-	yes	gardens, scenery
yes	some	-	yes	scenery, wildlife, sports facilities
yes	lots	-	yes	playground, scenery, walks
-	lots	yes	yes	camping, scenery, wildlife
-	little	-	-	scenery, views
yes	lots	-	yes	scenery, views
-	lots	yes	yes	camping, scenery
yes	lots	-	yes	playground, sports facilities
yes	lots	-	yes	gardens, scenery, walks
-	some	-	yes	gardens
-	lots	yes	yes	scenery, walks
yes	some	-	yes	playgrounds, scenery, walks
yes	lots	-	yes	playgrounds, scenery, walks
-	lots	-	yes	fishing, scenery, walks
yes	lots	yes	yes	playground, scenery, walks
yes	little	-	yes	scenery, walks
yes	lots	yes	yes	beach, scenery
yes	lots	yes	yes	scenery
-	lots	yes	yes	history, scenery, views, walks
yes	little	yes	yes	beach
yes	some	yes	yes	scenery
yes	some	yes	yes	boat ramp, scenery, walks
-	little	yes	yes	scenery, walks, things to do
-	some	yes	yes	scenery, walks, things to do
-	some	-	yes	scenery, views, walks
-	little	yes	yes	beach, history, scenery, walks
-	-	yes	-	beach, isolation, scenery, walks
-	some	yes	yes	beach, scenery, walks
-	little	yes	yes	beach, scenery, walks
-	lots	-	-	isolation, scenery, walks
yes	lots	-	yes	scenery

Sydney Botanic Gardens

City and Eastern Suburbs

Sydney's city is blessed with a remarkable string of ocean and harbour beaches. Long stretches of golden sand, some of the best surfing conditions in the world and a lively party vibe lights up ocean beaches such as Bondi, Coogee and Maroubra. Sheltered coves, pockets of bushland and city views grace the more sheltered harbour beaches such as Nielsen Park and Camp Cove.

Culture can be found in the clusters of music, theatre and dance companies at Walsh Bay and the Opera House, while some of the state's finest galleries and museums are situated near the Royal Botanic Gardens. On New Year's Eve, try grabbing a spot at Mrs Macquaries Point and watching the fireworks light up the sky. Or, for the more adventurous, why not sail or take a water taxi across the harbour to picnic on the tree-lined shores of Shark or Clark Island, with the backdrop of Sydney Harbour Bridge, Centrepoint Tower and the iconic sails of Sydney's Opera House.

The city from Watsons Bay (Robertson Park)

1 Royal Botanic Gardens

The Royal Botanic Gardens would be found high on any Sydneysider's list of ideal picnic destinations. The gardens (www.rbgsyd.nsw.gov.au) comprise of a meticulously maintained set of open spaces, ponds, walkways and various shady gardens on the western curve of Farm Cove. Free walking tours of the gardens are conducted daily at 1030 (not public holidays), meet at the information office. Adjacent to the gardens is Government House, the grounds of which are open daily 1000-1600 (see map, page 18).

At a glance

Address: Macquarie Street, Sydney

Map refs: G 346/B7, S 277/M16, U 236/G7 (plus see map, page 18)

Public transport: Circular Quay Ferry, Circular Quay/Martin Place Stations, buses to city centre

Parking: 1 hr metered in surrounding streets – public transport recommended

Entry fee: None

Opening times: 0700-1800 (2000 daylight saving)

BBQs: No

Boating: No

Dogs: No

Kiosk/café: Café in Middle Garden, open daily 0800-1630; Gardens Restaurant above (T 9241 2419) open daily 1200-1500 and for breakfast 0930-1130 Sat-Sun

Playground: No

Power/lights: Some street lighting

Shade: Many trees in park area

Swimming: No, but see opposite

Tables: No, some seating

Toilets: Yes, near café

Water: No

Wheelchairs: Toilet; good access

Mrs Macquaries Point

Mrs Macquaries Point, at the northern tip of the Domain, blends almost seamlessly into the Botanic Gardens. Grassy banks face the 'million-dollar' view of the Opera House and Harbour Bridge, and it's this view that makes the Point one of the most sought after spots on New Year's Eve (you'll need to arrive early in the day to get a prime position). Also in the Domain are an Olympic-standard pool and the impressive Art Gallery of NSW (see map, page 19).

At a glance

Address: The Domain, Mrs Macquaries Road, Sydney

Map refs: G 346/D5, S 277/P13, J 236/J5 (plus see map, page 18)

Public transport: Circular Quay Ferry, Circular Quay/Martin Place Stations, buses to city centre

Parking: 1 hr metered in surrounding streets – public transport recommended

Entry fee: None

Opening times: 24 hours

BBQs: No

Boating: No

Dogs: No

Kiosk/café: See opposite; also a café in the Andrew (Boy) Charlton Pool, open daily 0730-1500

Playground: No

Power/lights: Some street lighting

Shade: Many trees in park area

Swimming: Andrew (Boy) Charlton Pool (T 9358 6686), 300 m back from the Point, open daily 0600-1900 Oct-Apr (charges apply)

Tables: No, some seating

Toilets: Yes

Water: No

Wheelchairs: Toilet (in Botanic Gardens); good access

Sydney Opera House

Not only is the Opera House wonderful to look at, it's also fascinating to look around. Tours run every 30 minutes throughout the day, every day from 0900 to 1700 ($26, $23 if booked online and only $16 if you book a 0900, 0930 or 1000 tour online. There is also a VIP 'backstage' version that is more in-depth and finishes off with breakfast in the performers' café. This goes most days at 0700 for 2 hours ($140. T 9250 7111, www.sydneyoperahouse.com.

Government House and grounds

Adjacent to the Royal Botanic Gardens is Government House, the grounds of which are open daily 1000-1600. The house was completed in 1845 and is considered the foremost example of a Gothic revival building in the state. The suite of State Rooms contain some rare and well preserved 19th and 20th century furniture and decoration. Free tours of the house are run Fri-Sun, every 30 minutes from 1030-1500. Groups should book ahead, T 9931 5222.

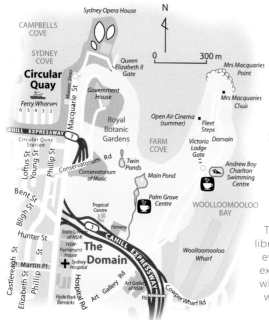

State Library of NSW

The State Library is something of a treasure house of books and documents many relating to the early history of New South Wales when it was a British colony. History and Heritage tours are available for groups of up to 20 (approximately 75 minutes). Bookings required, T 9273 1518. The Mitchell Wing of the library is devoted to an ever-changing series of exhibitions. To check out what's currently on, visit www.atmitchell.com.

Domain and Gardens

Hyde Park Barracks

Built by convict labour between 1817 and 1819, this is a popular landmark along Macquarie Street. Until 1848 it was the main convict barracks in New South Wales, providing lodgings for male convicts working on local government projects. On weekdays try to visit after 1500 to avoid school parties. Open daily 0930-1700, entrance $10, children $5. T 8239 2311, www.hht.net.au.

Art Gallery of New South Wales

This is the premier gallery in the state and sits in splendid isolation on Art Gallery Road in the southern part of the Domain. With strong collections of both Australian and European art, and spanning several centuries in a number of large open rooms, this is a must for any resident or visitor to Sydney with even half an interest in the arts. The gallery is free and open daily 1000-1700, to 2100 Weds; free highlight tours 1100, 1300 and 1400 Tues-Sun. The café and restaurant are both well situated to make the most of the gallery's northern views. T 9225 1744, www.artgallery.nsw.gov.au.

Andrew (Boy) Charlton Pool

Andrew 'Boy' Charlton was the most feted Australian swimmer for much of the first half of the twentieth century, and the Andrew Charlton pool is where his already growing reputation was cemented. He would surely be delighted to see how well cared for it now is, and would certainly enjoy the excellent facilities. The saltwater pool is heated and the complex includes a café, learners pool, therapy suites, terraced seating and sun deck. Pool entry $5.20, children $3.60. Summer only, T 9358 6686, www.abcpool.org.

3 Clark Island

Clark Island is just off Darling Point, and is one of only three harbour islands that allow informal visits. Facilities are modest, but access is limited both to numbers and ease of transport (no ferries), which make for a quiet getaway. The island is mostly covered in bushland, threaded with tracks and dotted with more open picnic areas. Visits have to be pre-booked and landing fees paid (T 9247 5033) as there is a limit on visitor numbers and the whole island may be booked for an event.

At a glance

Address: Sydney Harbour

Map refs: G 347/A7, S 278/E15, U 237/A7

Public transport: Only access by water taxi (1300 138840) or private boat

Entry fee: $5 landing fee per person

Opening times: 0800-1800 (2000 daylight saving)

BBQs: No

Boating: Yes!

Dogs: No

Kiosk/café: No

Playground: No

Power/lights: No

Shade: Many trees in park area

Swimming: Harbour, not recommended

Tables: Yes

Toilets: Yes

Water: Taps

Wheelchairs: Difficult access

4 Shark Island

At a glance

Address: Sydney Harbour

Map refs: G 347/G5, S 278/L13, U 237/G5

Public transport: Access by ferry (Matilda, T 9264 7377) from Circular Quay, water taxi, private boat – or hire canoes at Rose Bay (info@kayakhire.com.au)

Entry fee: $5 landing fee per person

Opening times: 0800-1800 (2000 daylight saving)

BBQs: No

Boating: Yes!

Dogs: No

Kiosk/café: No

Playground: No

Power/lights: No

Shade: Many trees in park area

Swimming: Harbour, not recommended

Tables: Yes

Toilets: Yes

Water: Taps

Wheelchairs: Difficult access

Just east of Clark Island, in the mouth of Rose Bay, Shark Island is larger and more open than Clark Island, and can also be reached by a regular ferry service. Named for its shape – not for any aquatic residents – it used to be an animal quarantine area until being handed over to form part of Sydney Harbour National Park in 1975. Facilities are also better than on Clark with picnic shelters and a small beach (swimming not recommended). Visits have to be pre-booked and landing fees paid (T 9247 5033) as there is a limit on visitor numbers and the whole island may be booked for an event.

5 Lyne Park

This is a popular park in Rose Bay thanks to the boat ramp, a very good children's playground and easy ferry access, though the large grassy area itself is somewhat scrubby. There are also tennis courts (T 9371 7122) and, just to the east beyond Woollahra Sailing Club, kayak hire (info@kayakhire.com.au). Alternatively, for those seeking a more adventurous, not to mention expensive activity, this is the location of the main jetty of Sydney Seaplanes (www.seaplanes.com.au) and Southern Cross Seaplanes (www.southerncrossseaplanes.com.au).

The playground at Lyne Park

At a glance

Address:
New South Head Road, Rose Bay

Map refs:
G 347/K10, S 278/P18, U 237/K10

Public transport: Rose Bay Ferry, buses 323, 324, 325

Parking: 2-4 hour restricted in car parks, unrestricted on main road

Entry fee: None

Opening times: 24 hours

BBQs: No

Boating: Boat ramp

Dogs: Off leash between 1630-0830, otherwise leashed

Kiosk/café: Lyne Park Café near eastern car park, a few others close by on New South Head Rd

Playground: Swings, climbing frame, ropes, slides; shaded

Power/lights: No

Shade: Small number of trees in park area

Swimming: Harbour beaches close by, not patrolled

Tables: A few

Toilets: Yes

Water: Bubbler by toilets

Wheelchairs: Toilet; good access

6 Strickland House,
Hermitage Foreshore Walk

At a glance

Address: Vaucluse Road, Vaucluse

Map refs: G 348/A3, S 278/Q12, U 237/L3

Public transport: Bus 325 stops at the end of Vaucluse Rd (400 m)

Parking: Unrestricted on Carrara and Vaucluse Rds

Entry fee: None

Opening times: 0500-2200

BBQs: No

Boating: No

Dogs: Off leash, but not on walk or beaches

Kiosk/café: Nearest a 10 min walk away at Shark Beach

Playground: No

Power/lights: No

Shade: Plenty of trees in park area

Swimming: Harbour beaches, not patrolled

Tables: One

Toilets: Yes (behind the main house)

Water: No

Wheelchairs: Good access to lawned area

The grounds of this recently renovated and very grand old house stretch right to the cliff edges and a small adjacent beach, and so encompass a stretch of the Hermitage Foreshore Walk. The garden is mostly an expanse of lawn but with plenty of trees for shade, and there is a commanding view right back down the harbour across Shark Island to the city. Facilities are sparse and this, together with the close, magnetic proximity of Shark Beach, almost guarantees a peaceful picnic.

ew from Strickland House lawns

7 Shark Beach and Nielsen Park

One of the city's most popular weekend destinations, this fine, sheltered (and netted) beach is lined by a promenade, with the large park behind offering the deep shade of mature fig trees. You can stretch your legs with a 300 metre loop walk out to the point or around to Hermit Bay. The main 'kiosk' is actually both an informal café/kiosk and doubles as a much sought after reception venue. Very busy in summer, keep Shark Beach in mind for a sunny winter's day.

At a glance

Address: Greycliffe Avenue, Vaucluse

Map refs: G 348/A1, S 278/Q9, U 237/L1

Public transport: Bus 325 stops at the end of Vaucluse Rd (400 m)

Parking: Unrestricted on local streets, usually very busy

Entry fee: None

Opening times: 24 hours

BBQs: No, portable gas BBQs are allowed

Boating: No

Dogs: No

Kiosk/café: Nielsen Park Kiosk (T 9337 1574), open daily

Playground: No

Power/lights: No

Shade: Plenty of trees on foreshore

Showers: No

Snorkelling: Yes

Surfing: No

Swimming: The whole beach is shark-netted in summer, not patrolled

Tables: Low platforms in Nielsen Park

Toilets: Yes

Water: Taps

Wheelchairs: Toilets; paved esplanade

8 Vaucluse Park

The grounds of Vaucluse House are beautifully maintained and contain a rare surviving example of a nineteenth century pleasure garden. Picnickers are allowed on the lawns (although resisting the tea-rooms

Vaucluse House

may be difficult). The house itself is owned by the Historic Houses Trust of NSW and is furnished in a style that reflects the mid 1800's when it was the home of explorer William Charles Wentworth. The house is open to the public Tues-Sun, 1000-1630 (T 9388 7922, www.hht.net.au). Patronising the tearooms gets you a 2-for-the-price-of-1 entry voucher to the house.

At a glance

Address: Wentworth Road, Vaucluse

Map refs: G 348/C3, S 279/A11, J 237/N3

Public transport: Bus 325 stops at the end of Vaucluse Rd (300 m)

Parking: Unrestricted car park open daily 1000-1700

Entry fee: None to grounds

Opening times: Daily 1000-1700

BQs: No

Boating: No

Dogs: Leashed

Kiosk/café: Vaucluse House Tearooms (T 9388 8188), open 1000-1600 Tues-Sun

Playground: No

Power/lights: No

Shade: Plenty of trees

Swimming: No

Tables: No

Toilets: Yes

Water: No

Wheelchairs: Toilet; good access to lawned areas

Parsley Bay is a narrow notch in the harbour foreshore, just west of Watsons Bay. It's a picturesque and popular reserve with an iron-span footbridge over a shallow beach. Behind lies a large grassy area and a very good – and shaded – children's playground. Plentiful tables, no dogs, lots of shady trees around the perimeter and a kiosk make this reserve particularly child-friendly.

At a glance

Address: Parsley Road, Vaucluse

Map refs: G 348/E2, S 279/C9, U 237/Q2

Public transport: Bus 325 stops on Hopetoun Ave (600 m)

Parking: Unrestricted car park closes at 1800 (2000 in summer)

Entry fee: None

Opening times: 24 hours

BBQs: No

Boating: No

Dogs: No

Kiosk/café: Parsley Bay Café, open daily 0900-1600

Playground: Swings, climbing frame, ropes, slides; mostly shaded by trees

Power/lights: No

Shade: Plenty of trees around park area

Swimming: Harbour beach, not patrolled

Tables: Many

Toilets: Yes

Water: Bubblers

Wheelchairs: Toilet; good access to lawned area

Relaxing at Parsley Bay

Robertson Park (Watsons Bay)

Watsons Bay is a favourite spot for Sydney visitors, primarily for the long ferry ride from the city, harbour views, the short walk to The Gap, and the long-established Doyles restaurant. The park lawn is separated from the narrow beach by a promenade and it's this lower area that becomes busiest with weekend visitors munching on their takeaway fish and chips. The playground and toilets are at the top of the park towards The Gap.

At a glance

Address: Military Road, Watsons Bay

Map refs: G 318/F14, S 279/D6, 218/A14

Public transport: Watsons Bay Ferry, buses 324, 325 stop on Military Rd (200 m)

Parking: Unrestricted in most nearby streets, but always very busy

Entry fee: None

Opening times: 24 hours

BBQs: No

Boating: No

Dogs: No

Kiosk/café: Several cafés; Doyles have a couple of restaurants here

(T 9337 2007) and the very popular fish & chip kiosk, but follow the promenade south for other good options and head up to the main road for gelato

Playground: Various unusual climbing frames, shaded

Power/lights: No

Shade: Some trees in park area

Swimming: Harbour beaches (not patrolled), and an enclosed harbour pool

Tables: A few

Toilets: Yes

Water: No

Wheelchairs: Toilet; good access

11 Camp Cove

This small golden crescent has views of the city and, although very popular, a slightly distant and secluded feel thanks to its position tucked inside South Head. Expensive houses sit right on the beachfront and 4WDs hustle for parking in the narrow streets of Watsons Bay, but there is plenty of space out on the bushy track to candy-striped Hornby Lighthouse.

At a glance

Address: Victoria Street, Watsons Bay

Map refs: G 318/E12, S 279/C4, U 217/Q12

Public transport: Rose Bay Ferry (500 m), buses 324, 325 stop on Military Rd (500 m)

Parking: Unrestricted, but very busy in nearby streets

Entry fee: No

Opening times: 24 hours

BBQs: No

Boating: No

Dogs: No

Kiosk/café: Kiosk open about 0800-1600 daily

Playground: No

Power/lights: No

Shade: Some trees on the grassy knoll at the western end

Showers: No

Snorkelling: Yes

Surfing: No

Swimming: Harbour, not patrolled

Tables: No

Toilets: Yes

Water: No

Wheelchairs: Limited access to beach

12 South Head

At a glance

Address: Watsons Bay (closest access from Cliff Street)

Map refs: G 318/F10, S 279/D1, U 218/A10

Public transport: Watsons Bay Ferry (1 km), buses 324, 325 stop on Military Rd (1 km)

Parking: Unrestricted, but very busy in nearby streets

Entry fee: None

Opening times: 24 hours

BBQs: No

Boating: No

Dogs: No

Kiosk/café: Nearest at Camp Cove

Playground: No

Power/lights: No

Shade: Small number of trees in park area

Swimming: No

Tables: No

Toilets: Near Lady Bay

Water: At toilet block near Lady Bay

Wheelchairs: Difficult access

Naturally there are impressive views from South Head and this makes it a popular picnic destination despite the lack of facilities. The headland is part of the Sydney Harbour National Park and has some interesting old fortifications, although much of the area is closed off (it's an operating naval base: HMAS Watson). There are some grassy areas around the lighthouse keeper's cottage and also lots of large flat boulders to sit on. The location is quite exposed so it's not a good choice on a windy day.

Lighthouse keepers cottage

13 Centennial Park

For many Sydneysiders, Centennial Park is a place of memories: of childhood adventures, family picnics, illicit midnight swims and stolen kisses. Dedicated to the people by Sir Henry Parkes in 1888, this masterpiece of urban planning is an island of calm in the hurley-burley of city life. Dotted with huge old trees, historic pavilions, low hills and duck-covered ponds, this is a park where there is always something new to discover.

Today, Centennial Park is a haven for cyclists, horse-riders, fitness fanatics and golden labradors. For the purists who bemoan the passing of these grand times, the car-free days on the last Sunday of every season are the time to visit: check out www.cp.nsw.gov.au for dates.

At a glance

Address: Lang Road, Centennial Park

Map refs: G 376/H4, S 298/B8, U 256/N4

Public transport: Closest bus 355 stops on Cook Rd (400 m), also buses 352, 378, 380 along Oxford St

Parking: Unrestricted

Entry fee: None

Opening times: 24 hours for pedestrians, sunrise to sunset for vehicles

BBQs: Yes, electric

Booking: Required for groups of 50 or more, T 9939 6699

Dogs: Leashed and unleashed areas

Kiosk/café: A la carte restaurant and café open 08 30—1530 7 days. Also kiosk at Duck Pond, weekends

Playground: There are three playgrounds, including a Learners Cycleway and wheelchair-accessible swing

Power/lights: Yes

Shade: Significant tree plantings, ample shade

Swimming: No

Tables: Yes

Toilets: Yes

Water: Bubblers throughout the park

Wheelchairs: Toilets: parking; accessible nature trail, liberty swing

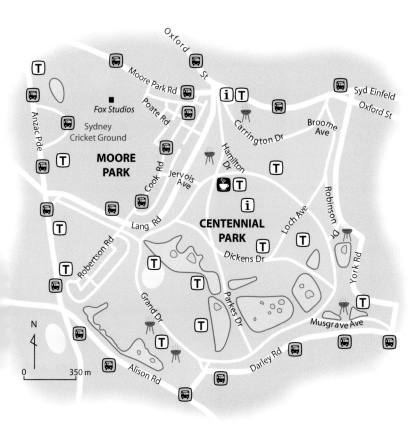

Sydney history – Centennial Park

Centennial Park was once a huge area of creeks and swampland, fed by ground water and sheltered by tall paperbarks. In the early years of settlement, the area was known as Second Sydney Common, and in 1920, an area called Lachlan Water Reserve was set aside for Sydney's future water supplies. In 1825, when Sydney's original water supply became foul and almost ran dry — history does have a tendency to repeat itself, after all — a surveyor called John Busby used convict labour to build a 3.5 kilometre underground tunnel that led all the way to Hyde Park, drawing water from a series of dams from the water reserve.

Grazing and poor management gradually meant that the water in the swamps became polluted and by the late 1800s, the dams were changed to become the ponds that still exist today. In 1888, on the centenary of European settlement, Sir Henry Parkes dedicated the area to become one of Sydney's first public parks and in the years that followed, hundreds of unemployed labourers were enlisted to fulfill this vision.

By the time Federation of Australia came to pass, on January 1, 1901, Centennial Park had been transformed and thousands of people gathered to celebrate at the Federation Pavilion.

14 Cooper Park

This steep-sided, bush-covered valley is a surprising find so close to Bondi Junction. The floor of the valley is taken up by several tennis courts (you'll find court, ball and racquet hire at the kiosk), but beyond these are a children's playground and quiet, shaded picnic areas. A narrow creek murmurs alongside which, while adding to the romantic setting, is clearly a breeding opportunity for mosquitoes. Several short bushtracks lead up and away from the picnic area.

Bush track in Cooper Park

At a glance

Address: Suttie Road, Woollahra

Map refs: G 377/D1, S 298/J5, U 257/F1

Public transport: Bondi Junction Station (400 m), the 327 bus stops close to the main entrance, many buses go to Bondi Junction

Parking: Unrestricted car park

Entry fee: None

Opening times: 24 hours

BBQs: No

Boating: No

Dogs: Leashed

Kiosk/café: Open at least 0700-2000 daily

Playground: Swings, climbing frame, ropes

Power/lights: No

Shade: Plenty of trees in picnic area

Swimming: No

Tables: A few

Toilets: Yes

Water: Bubblers

Wheelchairs: Toilet; good access to picnic area

Clifftop walks in the eastern suburbs

It is possible to walk along the clifftops and beaches all the way from South Head to La Perouse. The best known of these walks is the Bondi to Coogee stretch (6 kilometres one way) which every Sydneysider should do at least once — and every visitor who is given the chance – but Dover Heights to The Gap (5 kilometres one way) is almost its equal and far less busy. Coogee to Maroubra (5 kilometres one way) is an interesting walk along low cliffs and suburban back streets, while Maroubra to La Perouse (10.5 kilometres one way) heads away from suburbia around the borders of the Anzac Rifle Range and three golf courses. All are detailed in the companion walking guide, *Sydney's Best Harbour & Coastal Walks* published by Woodslane Press.

Looking north to Diamond Bay, just east of Vaucluse Park

Mackenzies Point, just south of Bondi

Early morning on the beach

At a glance

Address: Campbell Parade, Bondi

Map refs: G 378/E3, S 299/C7, U 257/Q3

Public transport: Buses 361, 380 (from the city), 381 and 382

Parking: Expensive adjacent car parks; nearest streets are 2-4 hour metered, 2-4 hour restricted about 200 m further back from Campbell Pde

Entry fee: None

Opening times: 24 hours

BBQs: Electric in Biddigal Reserve at eastern end 40 cents/15 mins (20 cent coins)

Boating: No

Dogs: Leashed on promenade

Kiosk/café: Some near the central pavilion, many along Campbell Pde

Playground: Just east of pavilion; Skate park at western end

Power/lights: Street lighting

Shade: Sheltered tables by BBQ, on the foreshore lawns at the western end and near pavilion

Showers: Along promenade

Snorkelling: At eastern end

Surfing: Yes

Swimming: Ocean, patrolled; rock baths at both ends of the beach (charges apply at icebergs)

Tables: Many

Toilets: Yes (pavilion & icebergs)

Water: No

Wheelchairs: Toilets (pavilion); paved Esplanade

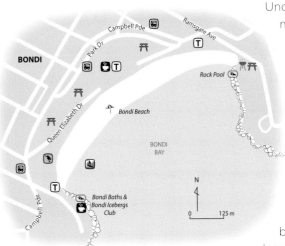

Undoubtedly Sydney's most famous and busiest beach, Bondi has a long wide sweep of sand below a hilly suburb bristling with apartment blocks. It's always thronged with tourists, visitors and beautiful bronzed locals drawn by the golden sand, rolling surf and vibrant energy. Bondi is definitely 'where it's at'. There is lots of grass above the beach, very good picnic facilities and some above-average markets on a Sunday. Bondi is an ideal beach to take your first surfing lessons. Check out www.adrenalin. com.au for details. No alcohol in public areas.

The Icebergs pool

Sydney history – The Icebergs

The Bondi Icebergs is a swimming club founded in 1929 by a few hardy men who wanted to stay fit during winter. They drew up a constitution featuring a rule of membership that stated swimmers must compete on three Sundays out of four for five years. Women were allowed to join in 1994 and there are now about 350 thick-skinned members. The club celebrates the start of the winter swimming season on the first Sunday in May by throwing blocks of ice into the pool.

16 Tamarama Beach

This small but almost perfectly formed beach is sometimes referred to as 'Glamourama', which tells you all you need to know about how well to do the locals are! It has good surf, a café and a pleasant, open park. Steps down from the road give very direct access to the water so it's also a good beach for a quick swim, so long as you watch out for the rips for which this beach is notorious. No alcohol in public areas.

At a glance

Address: Pacific Avenue, Tamarama

Map refs: G 378/B7, S 298/R11, U 257/M7

Public transport: Buses 361, 380 (from the city) and 381

Parking: Unrestricted in nearby streets

Entry fee: None

Opening times: 24 hours

BBQs: Electric (20 cent coins)

Boating: No

Dogs: Leashed on promenade, or on rock platforms at northern end

Kiosk/café: Tamarama Beach Café open daily 0900-1700

Playground: Swings

Power/lights: No

Shade: Sheltered tables

Showers: Yes

Snorkelling: No

Surfing: Yes (closed to boards during patrol hours)

Swimming: Ocean, patrolled

Tables: Many

Toilets: Yes

Water: Bubblers and taps

Wheelchairs: Toilets; paved esplanade

One of the prettiest beaches in the eastern suburbs, Bronte is a small surf beach with white sands, flanked by a large park with pockets of bushland and a strip of excellent cafes along Bronte Rd. When the wind gets up, the rips at Bronte Beach can be very dangerous — no guessing how the rip 'Tamarama Express' gets its name — but the Bogey Hole, a natural tidal rock pool at the southern end, provides safe swimming in all weather conditions, as does the nearby ocean pool.

At a glance

Address: Bronte Road, Bronte

Map refs: G 378/B9, S 298/Q13, J 257/L9

Public transport: Buses 360, 361 and 378 (from the city)

Parking: 1 hour metered on Bronte Rd, other streets unrestricted

Entry fee: None

Opening times: 24 hours

BBQs: Many electric (20 cent coins)

Boating: No

Dogs: Leashed on promenade

Kiosk/café: Bronte Kiosk open 0900-1700, other cafés on Bronte Rd

Playground: Swings, slides, climbing frames, plus a miniature railway track on weekends ($2 per ride)

Power/lights: No

Shade: Many sheltered tables, some trees

Showers: Yes

Snorkelling: No

Surfing: Yes

Swimming: Ocean, patrolled; rock baths at southern end

Tables: Many

Toilets: Yes

Water: Bubblers and taps

Wheelchairs: Toilets; paved esplanade

18 Coogee Beach

Coogee is a lively suburban beach with a huge pub on the foreshore strip amid a jumble of apartments and hotels. Smaller and, let's be honest, a little less fashionable than Bondi, it's also less pretentious. Coogee stands out for its collection of rock baths and headland walks particularly the one south to Trenery Reserve. All this, plus some interesting rocks and accessible snorkelling at the northern end, make Coogee a great family beach. No alcohol in public areas after dark.

At a glance

Address: Arden Street, Coogee

Map refs: G 377/H16, S 298/M20, U 257/H16

Public transport: Buses 313, 314, 370, 372, 373 and 374

Parking: Metered car park at northern end; streets restricted to 30 mins – 4 hrs

Entry fee: None

Opening times: 24 hours

BBQs: Electric (free) at northern end

Boating: No

Dogs: Leashed on promenade

Kiosk/café: Many on Arden St

Playground: At Grant Reserve (see p 39)

Power/lights: Street lighting

Shade: A few trees, sheltered tables near BBQs

Showers: Yes

Snorkelling: At northern end

Surfing: Yes, small breaks only

Swimming: Ocean, patrolled; rock pools at southern end

Tables: Yes

Toilets: Yes

Water: Bubblers

Wheelchairs: Paved esplanade

At a glance

Address: Beach Street, Coogee

Map refs: G 407/H2, S 318/M2, U 277/H2

Public transport: Buses 313, 314, 370, 372, 373 and 374 stop in Coogee (300 m)

Parking: 4 hr restricted on Beach St

Entry fee: None

Opening times: 24 hours

BBQs: Electric (free)

Boating: No

Dogs: Leashed

Kiosk/café: In Coogee (300 m)

Playground: Swings, climbing frames, rope pyramid, flying fox

Power/lights: No

Shade: Some trees around picnic areas

Swimming: McIver Baths (women & children only), also Wylies Rock Baths

Tables: Yes

Toilets: Yes

Water: Taps

Wheelchairs: Good access to picnic areas

Up on the headland, just south of Coogee Beach, Grant Reserve offers a quieter alternative to the usually busy beach foreshore. At the northern end of the large grassy playing field is a very good playground, some tables and BBQs and the McIver Baths at the northern end, with a handful of tables and BBQs at the southern end. McIver Baths are, it is thought, unique in Australia in being the last remaining pool for women and children only.

Playground at Grant Reserve

The southernmost of the main eastern beaches, Maroubra is also marginally the longest at just over a kilometre long. The southern end, surrounded by bushland, is quieter than the more suburban north end, so even if it's busy there is still plenty of opportunity to get away from the crowds. Maroubra has a lively surf culture, with consistent beach breaks in most conditions, and became Australia's first ever National Surfing Reserve in 2006. Sydney Safe Surf School operates here, T 9365 4370.

At a glance

Address: Marine Parade, Maroubra

Map refs: G 407/G13, S 318/L13, U 277/G13

Public transport: Buses 317, 353, 376, 377, 395 and 396

Parking: 4 hr metered in main car park, unrestricted in nearby Broome St

Entry fee: None

Opening times: 24 hours

BBQs: Electric (free) behind Pavilion

Boating: No

Dogs: Leashed on promenade

Kiosk/café: Pavilion Café faces the beach, a kiosk is at the rear (daily from 0800 to 2000 if busy); others along Marine Pde

Playground: Climbing frames, slides; shaded; excellent skate park

Power/lights: Some street lighting

Shade: A few trees, sheltered tables near BBQs

Showers: Yes

Snorkelling: No

Surfing: Yes, home to the 'Bra Boys

Swimming: Ocean, patrolled

Tables: Yes

Toilets: Yes

Water: Taps

Wheelchairs: Toilets; paved esplanade

21 Sir Joseph Banks Park

the heart of the Botany industrial area, and right alongside reshore Road, this park looks uninviting on a map. In reality the gh banks and trees reduce the road noise to a low hum and signs industry are nonexistent. Bushland hugs the banks of a series of turesque ponds where you'll find ducks and geese; there are my shady walks, gardens and a 'zoo playground' with lifesize mal sculptures. Among many single-table shelters there is one ge shelter with several tables and BBQs.

t a glance

ddress: Fremlin Street, Botany

ap refs: G 435/H1, S 317/H17, U)6/C1

ublic transport: Bus 309 stops on ptany Rd (400 m)

arking: Unrestricted car park, oses 1900

ntry fee: None

pening times: 24 hours

BQs: Electric (free)

oating: No

Dogs: Leashed

Kiosk/café: No

Playground: Swings, animal sculptures, slides

Power/lights: No

Shade: Trees around picnic areas, sheltered tables

Swimming: No

Tables: Yes

Toilets: Yes

Water: Taps

Wheelchairs: Good access to picnic areas

e main pond

22 Frenchmans Bay and Yarra Bay

These two beaches are right opposite Port Botany Container Terminal, which doesn't sound all that exciting, but the attractions of the area are a pleasant surprise. The beaches themselves are spacious and clean, with a beachside café on the southern end. Watching the container ships come in and out of Botany Bay and the planes taking off from the airport can be fascinating to many children (and adults). Plus there are two museums well worth a visit (see opposite).

At a glance

Address: Endeavour Avenue, Frenchmans Bay

Map refs: G 436/J14, S 338/C10, U 296/P14

Public transport: Buses 391, 393 and 394

Parking: Unrestricted in local streets

Entry fee: None

Opening times: 24 hours

BBQs: One electric (free)

Boating: No

Dogs: No

Kiosk/café: Boatshed Café open 0900-1630 Tues-Sun (T 9661 9315); others just beyond the foreshore

Playground: Swing

Power/lights: No

Shade: Some sheltered tables, a few foreshore trees

Showers: No

Snorkelling: Yes

Surfing: No

Swimming: Harbour, not patrolled

Tables: Yes

Toilets: Yes

Water: No

Wheelchairs: Not good access

Frenchmans Bay

Out and about
in La Perouse

La Perouse is named after Jean-François de Galaup, Comte de la Perouse, who was the commander of a French expedition to explore the Pacific. He sailed into Botany Bay on the very day that the First Fleet was leaving it and spent six weeks in the area. La Perouse Museum and Visitor Centre, in the Cable Station building, contains maps, antique scientific instruments and relics recovered from the wrecks of La Perouse's frigates Boussole and Astrolabe. T 9311 3379. Open Wed-Sun 1000-1600. A fort was built on the little island opposite in 1885 when the Crimean war made Sydneysiders feel vulnerable to the threat of Russian invasion. The NPWS runs Bare Island Fort tours on Sundays: meet at the fort entrance. Booking in advance is not necessary. T 9247 5033. Sun 1330, 1430, $7.70 adults, $5.50 children, $22 families.

Bare Island

here are two other beaches in the Botany area, just over the headland from enchmans Bay: Congwong Bay Beach and Little Congwong Beach, both part of e Botany Bay National Park and surrounded by dense bushland. There are no cilities at either but that means they are likely to be less busy and quite possibly eserted. They aren't great on a windy day, but are a good pick on a calm, sunny ternoon. Following the signposted walking track at the far end of Congwong Bay each will take you to Endeavour Lightstation on Henry Head in about 20 minutes.

ongwong Bay Beach

Near West

Once you're west of the Harbour Bridge, the waters of Port Jackson narrow, meandering past inner city suburbs to where Parramatta River meets Lane Cove River. Deep bays continue to spread away from the main channel on either side, and from many vantage points it becomes difficult to work out which are the bays and which is the main channel. Most of the picnic spots in this section are on the foreshore of the diminishing harbour, or on the banks of Cooks, Lane Cove and Parramatta Rivers. Almost all offer harbour or river views that contrast strongly with the better known vistas from the Lower North Shore and the city.

Some of the parks in this area have only recently been reclaimed and landscaped, having formerly been the sites of industrial buildings or works. It is likely that a future edition of this book will carry an entry for Ballast Point in Birchgrove. This former Caltex oil terminal is undergoing the process that some of these parks, including Pyrmont Point, have already undergone.

Canal near Bicentennial Park, Glebe

23 Gough Whitlam Park

This large grassy area nestles in a bend on the Cooks River, not far from where it widens out adjacent to Sydney Airport. This well laid-out park has several large grassy areas, a set of decorative ponds, plenty of tall trees, two playgrounds and a riverside walk. All the BBQs are wood, however, except for two adjacent to the car park.

At a glance

Address: Bayview Avenue, Undercliffe

Map refs: G 404/J3, S 316/E2, U 274/P2

Public transport: Tempe Station (400 m), buses 422 and 425 stop on Princes Hwy (600 m)

Parking: Unrestricted car park

Entry fee: None

Opening times: 24 hours

BBQs: Electric (free) near car park, wood beyond the ponds (wood provided)

Boating: No

Dogs: Leashed

Kiosk/café: No

Playground: Swings, climbing frame, ropes, slides; basketball court

Power/lights: No

Shade: Plenty of trees, some sheltered tables

Swimming: Not recommended

Tables: Yes

Toilets: Yes

Water: Bubbler by toilets

Wheelchairs: Toilet; good access

Bowls practice

24 Ewen Park

A little further up Cooks River from Gough Whitlam Park, and also adjacent to the river, Ewen Park is much smaller but does have a similar feel. BBQs and tables are scattered throughout the park and clever landscaping helps create an air of privacy. No alcohol is allowed in the park at any time.

At a glance

Address:
Tennent Parade, Hurlstone Park

Map refs: G 373/B14, S 295/N19, U 254/F14

Public transport: Hurlstone Park Station (500 m), bus 409 (200 m)

Parking: Unrestricted on adjacent road

Entry fee: None

Opening times: 24 hours

BBQs: Electric (free)

Boating: No

Dogs: Leashed

Kiosk/café: No

Playground: Swings, climbing frame, slides

Power/lights: No

Shade: Some trees, some sheltered tables

Swimming: Not recommended

Tables: Yes

Toilets: Yes, behind soccer club house

Water: Taps

Wheelchairs: Good access

25 Peace Park

This modest suburban hill is just high enough — and has been kept sufficiently clear of buildings — to afford extensive views to the south and west (the Blue Mountains are visible on a clear day). The recently built lookout extends this view to include glimpses of the city itself including the Sydney Harbour Bridge. Facilities are modest, but the well-kept, rolling slope of grass, dotted here and there with young trees, is as inviting a spot as any for a picnic blanket.

The view from the lookout

At a glance

Address: Trevenar Street, Ashbury

Map refs: G 372/H7, S 295/K11, U 254/C7

Public transport: Ashfield Station (1.3 km), buses 413, 471 and 472

Parking: Unrestricted car park

Entry fee: None

Opening times: 24 hours

BBQs: Electric (free)

Boating: No

Dogs: Leashed

Kiosk/café: No

Playground: Climbing frame, slides; shaded

Power/lights: No

Shade: A few trees, some sheltered tables

Swimming: No

Tables: Yes

Toilets: Yes

Water: No

Wheelchairs: Good access

At a glance

Address: Pirrama Road, Pyrmont

Map refs: G 345/C7, S 277/C15, U 235/N7

Public transport: John St Square Metro Light Rail station (400 m), buses 443 and 449 stop at Star City (400 m)

Parking: Street parking metered 0600-2330

Entry fee: None

Opening times: 24 hours

BBQs: Electric (free)

Boating: No

Dogs: Off leash

Kiosk/café: No

Playground: Slide, swings, interesting climbing frames

Power/lights: Street lighting

Shade: A few trees, two sheltered tables

Swimming: No

Tables: Yes

Toilets: Yes

Water: Bubblers

Wheelchairs: Toilet, good access

Perched at the end of Pyrmont, this fairly small park benefits from a lack of nearby traffic, even on a busy weekday. A lawned area is fringed by a timber jetty and walkway and, further to the west, a playground and interesting sculpture area. There are views over to Balmain, the Anzac Bridge and the Glebe Island car terminal.

Part of a surprisingly large recreational area that also includes Federal Park and Harold Park Raceway, several large grassy areas are separated by avenues of trees, paths and cycleways, and dotted with many large fig trees. The 'Bicentennial' part is adjacent to Rozelle Bay, and though spacious does not allow unleashed dogs (which can be exercised in Federal Park when there are no sports going on). The playground is comprehensive and includes a rare roundabout. No alcohol is allowed at any time.

At a glance

Address: Eglinton Road, Glebe

Map refs: G 344/H12, S 276/P20, U 235/H12

Public transport: Jubilee Metro Light Rail station (200 m), buses 432 and 433 stop at Glebe Point (100 m)

Parking: Some unrestricted on nearby roads

Entry fee: None

Opening times: 24 hours

BBQs: No

Boating: No

Dogs: Off leash area, otherwise leashed

Kiosk/café: No

Playground: Slide, swings, climbing frame, roundabout

Power/lights: Some street lighting

Shade: Many trees, sheltered tables

Swimming: Not recommended

Tables: Yes

Toilets: Yes, near oval

Water: Bubblers

Wheelchairs: Good access

28 Leichhardt Park & Callan Park

Between them these large, mostly green areas comprise a large stretch of the much-loved Iron Cove 'Bay Run' that follows the entire shore of Iron Cove. Facilities are minimal, but there are many harbourside spots to spread a blanket and drop a basket. A stroll around the grounds of Rozelle Hospital and the Sydney College of the Arts (Callan Park) is quite fascinating, the buildings varying from well-maintained Victorian Italianate to abandoned Federation weatherboard. Although protected from development, the future of much of the park is still uncertain. Check out www.callanpark.com for more information.

At a glance

Address: Glover Street & Wharf Road, Lilyfield

Map refs: G 343/J9, S 276/E18, J 234/P9

Public transport: The 440 and 445 stop on Perry St (400m)

Parking: Unrestricted car parks and in nearby streets

Entry fee: None

Opening times: 24 hours

BBQs: No

Boating: No

Dogs: Leashed in Leichhardt Park, off leash in Callan

Kiosk/café: In Aquatic Centre

Playground: No

Power/lights: No

Shade: Many trees

Swimming: Aquatic Centre in Leichhardt Park, open daily 0530-2000, charges apply

Tables: Very few, more in Aquatic Centre

Toilets: In Aquatic Centre

Water: Bubblers/taps

Wheelchairs: Good access

This small harbourside park comprises a large sloping lawn with picnic and BBQ facilities at the top and the wonderful Viking ship play area at the bottom. Fringed completely with trees, there are also some interesting sculptures dotted around the place. The park commemorates the poet Henry Lawson, who lived nearby on Great North Road in the 1920s. If coming by public transport alight at the ferry wharf and walk around the foreshore through Battersea Park and Quarantine Reserve.

At a glance

Address: St Albans Street, Abbotsford

Map refs: G 342/J2, S 275/K9, U 234/C2

Public transport: Abbotsford Ferry (500 m), the 438 bus stops on Great North Rd (500 m) and at the ferry wharf

Parking: Unrestricted on nearby streets

Entry fee: None

Opening times: 24 hours

BBQs: Electric (free)

Boating: No

Dogs: Off leash

Kiosk/café: No

Playground: Slide, swings, Viking ship climbing and activity area

Power/lights: No

Shade: A few trees, sheltered tables

Swimming: Not recommended

Tables: Yes

Toilets: No

Water: Bubblers/taps

Wheelchairs: Difficult access

Popular for its boat ramp, Bayview Park initially strikes you as all car park, but a glance to the right as you walk or drive in reveals a grassy stretch down to the shore that's mostly out of sight of the vehicles. This is well-shaded, has a good playground, and there's the option of a long waterside stroll in either direction.

At a glance

Address: Burwood Road, Canada Bay

Map refs: G 342/G5, S 275/J13, J 234/DB5

Public transport: Bayview Park Ferry, buses 502 and 463

Parking: Car park from $1 per hour, locked at 1800 (2000 during daylight saving); unrestricted in local streets

Entry fee: None

Opening times: 24 hours

BBQs: Electric (free)

Boating: Boat ramp

Dogs: Off leash

Kiosk/café: No

Playground: Slides, climbing frame

Power/lights: No

Shade: Many trees, sheltered tables

Swimming: Not recommended

Tables: Yes

Toilets: Yes

Water: Taps

Wheelchairs: Good access

31 Prince Edward Park, Cabarita

This harbourside park manages to pack some varied topography and facilities into a very small area. A modest grassy area crowns a low hillock which is fringed by trees, mangroves, a playground, sheltered seating and BBQs. Beyond the trees is a pleasant foreshore walkway that continues south right around Exile Bay to Bayview Park (see previous page). A prominent feature of the park is the carefully designed restaurant, Angelo's, and facilities building near the entrance

At a glance

Address: Phillips Street, Cabarita

Map refs: G 342/F3, S 275/H11, U 234/A3

Public transport: Buses 462 and 466 stop at the end of Phillips St (500 m)

Parking: Car park restricted to 3 hrs to 1800 Mon-Fri and to 1230 Sat-Sun

Entry fee: None

Opening times: 24 hours

BBQs: Electric (free)

Boating: No

Dogs: Leashed

Kiosk/café: Part of (but underneath the well-regarded Angelo's restaurant (T 9743 2225), open Tues-Sun from midday

Playground: Pirate ship climbing frame

Power/lights: No

Shade: Many trees, sheltered seatin

Swimming: Not recommended

Tables: No

Toilets: Yes, by kiosk

Water: Taps and bubblers

Wheelchairs: Good access

Despite some pretty gardens and a rare beach for this part of the harbour, Cabarita Park is most popular for the pool complex that sits on the foreshore overlooking the entrance to Hen & Chicken Bay. It has modest entry charges, a variety of heated outdoor pools, including one of an Olympic standard, a sheltered lawned area and boardwalk sun-traps. The park itself has a few grassy areas, plenty of shady trees and several sheltered tables.

At a glance

Address: Cabarita Road, Cabarita

Map refs: G 312/E15, S 275/H7, U 214/A15

Public transport: Cabarita Ferry, bus 466

Parking: Car park from $1 per hour; unrestricted in local streets

Entry fee: None

Opening times: 24 hours

BBQs: Electric (free)

Boating: No

Dogs: Leashed

Kiosk/café: Kiosk at the small marina and at the pool (pool entry not required)

Playground: Slide, climbing frame

Power/lights: No

Shade: Many trees, one very large shelter with multiple tables, other sheltered tables

Swimming: Olympic pool (open Sept-April, 0600 to 1800 or later, T 9743 2326); modest beach

Tables: Yes

Toilets: Yes, near entrance and at pool (pool entry not required)

Water: Taps and bubblers

Wheelchairs: Good access

33 Bicentennial Park, Sydney Olympic Park

Bicentennial Park is a testimony to what can happen when political willpower, federal funds and the vision of the public combine to create something very special. There are picnic areas throughout the 40 hectares of landscaped parklands, everything from secluded grassy patches near Lake Belvedere to large shelters with electric BBQs that accommodate up to 200 people. It's easy to combine a picnic with a little exercise: walkways and cycleways stretch north through mangroves, saltmarsh and wetland, leading to a secluded bird hide. Children love the paths and cycleways, and also the two playgrounds and the sheer joy of getting wet in any one of the 200 fountains below the Treillage Tower! Bike hire, next to Lilies on the Park café, has a large range of bikes, mountain bikes, adult trikes, tandems, kid's bikes and have child carriers (open daily 0900-1700, T 9714 7888).

At a glance

Address: Australia Avenue, Homebush Bay

Map refs: G 341/A2, S 274/J10, U 380/N16

Public transport: Concord West Station (500 m), bus 525 stops on Underwood Rd (800 m), or RiverCat to Sydney Olympic Park Wharf (bus 401 connects with the ferry into the park)

Parking: Unrestricted, closed at sunset

Entry fee: None

Opening times: Sunrise to sunset

Bookings: Yes. Suitable for groups of 30 to 200, open spaces $62.50, pavilions $120, T 9714 7524. BBQ areas cannot be booked

BBQs: Electric (free) at Lake Belvedere, Village Green and Concord West picnic areas

Boating: No

Dogs: Leashed (not in the wetlands)

Kiosk/café: Lilies on the Park café (open 0730 to 1700), Bel Parco Ristorante (open lunch and dinner)

Playground: Two, and they're excellent

Power/lights: Yes

Shade: Lots of shelters suitable for small groups; several large shelters/pavilions

Swimming: No

Tables: Yes

Toilets: Yes

Water: Taps and bubblers

Wheelchairs: Toilets; good access; Liberty swing at the Village Green

33 Bicentennial Park, Sydney Olympic Park

Out and about - Sydney Olympic Park

Positioned on 640 hectares of land sandwiched between Parramatta River and the M4, Sydney Olympic Park is one of the world's most significant urban renewal projects. Even if you don't want to buy a ticket to one of the sporting events there, or you're averse to the big crowds at events such as the Royal Easter Show, it's well worth just visiting the park to have a wander around.

Renewal of the site began during the 1980s and culminated with the success of the Sydney Olympics in 2000. Now, nearly two thirds of the site is parkland, but this parkland surrounds not only a large number of sporting facilities and large venues, but also several open public spaces such as Olympic Plaza and Olympic Boulevard. Solar lighting towers, fountains, cohesive landscaping and several large-scale permanent art installations all combine to create a striking urban landscape.

Probably the best way to explore the park is on a bike, but if you're on foot, start at the visitor centre (close Olympic Park railway station), explore the public spaces near Acer Arena and then cycle down to the Brickpit Ring Walk. This circuit gives a good impression of the sheer scale of the Olympic Park project.

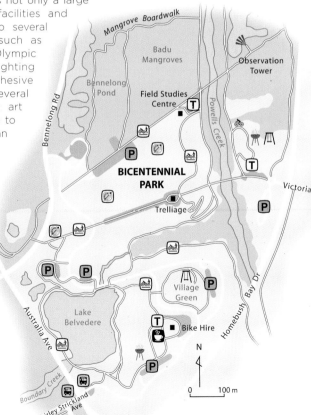

34 George Kendall Riverside Reserve

This reserve is mostly a huge expanse of grass, laid out as playing fields and hence perfect for large games of footy, softball, cricket, etc. The addition of basketball and tennis courts (bookings, T 9638 6368), plus good BBQ and picnic facilities, make this a destination worth considering for any large sporting group or family, as does the fact that it can be quite deserted even on days which would see other parks very busy.

At a glance

Address: Boyle Street, Ermington

Map refs: G 310/E5, S 254/C17, U 212/K5

Public transport: Buses 520, 523 and 524 stop on Victoria Rd (700 m)

Parking: Unrestricted car park

Entry fee: None

Opening times: 24 hours

Bookings: T 9806 5140 for a shelter with 3 tables and 2 BBQs

BBQs: Electric (free)

Boating: No

Dogs: Off leash

Kiosk/café: No

Playground: Swings, slides, climbin frame; basketball courts; tennis courts

Power/lights: No

Shade: Sheltered tables

Swimming: No

Tables: Yes

Toilets: Yes, at rear of the 'meeting room'

Water: Bubblers

Wheelchairs: Good access

Meadowbank Memorial Park

Although this park is quite large, the main picnic area is relatively modest. Small grassy areas are dotted along the foreshore with a playground, tables and BBQs set further back and up the slope. This area is particularly well sheltered with many trees. Children love the bike track that runs alongside the Parramatta River through the park. Another interesting feature is the WWII Memorial Walk which has been constructed using stones from each country where Australians served.

At a glance

Address: Bank Street, West Ryde

Map refs: G 311/D5, S 254/M17, U 213/D5

Public transport: Meadowbank Station (300 m), Meadowbank Ferry, bus 513 goes to the ferry wharf

Parking: Unrestricted car park

Entry fee: None

Opening times: 24 hours

BBQs: Electric (free)

Boating: No

Dogs: Leashed

Kiosk/café: No

Playground: Slides, climbing frame; basketball hoop

Power/lights: No

Shade: Sheltered tables

Swimming: Not recommended

Tables: Yes

Toilets: Yes

Water: Taps

Wheelchairs: Good access

36 Lane Cove National Park

The picturesque stretch of river at Lane Cove National Park makes for a great day out for families, with dozens of picnic spots dotted either side of the river. Facilities include a kiosk, visitor centre and a boatshed from where you can hire rowboats, canoes and pedal boats. Just behind the kiosk, there's also the Kukundi wildlife shelter, a good place to have a close-up look at flying foxes, tawny frogmouth owls and other local fauna (admission free, open 1000-1500). For lots of additional information on the park see users.bigpond.net.au/folcnp.

At a glance

Address: Access from Delhi Road or Lady Game Drive, Chatswood West

Map refs: G 283/F8, S 256/B3, U 194/L8

Public transport: Buses 259, 545 and 550 stop by Fullers Bridge

Entry fee: $7 per vehicle (free with NPWS pass)

Opening times: 0900 to 1800 (1900 daylight saving)

Bookings: Only for groups of 40 or more Jan to Oct, 80 or more Nov and Dec; booking fee $65 upwards (T 9888 9160)

BBQs: Some gas (free), many wood (wood not supplied)

Boating: Canoe/kayak hire at Lane Cove Boatshed, from $20 per hour (open 1200-1700 Sat-Sun, T 0418 600695)

Camping: At Lane Cove River Touris[t] Park, T 9888 9133, www.lanecoverivertouristpark.com.a[u]

Dogs: No

Kiosk/café: Kookaburra Kiosk, Lad[y] Game Dr (open Sat-Sun 1030 to 1700 T 9410 0155)

Playground: Climbing frames, slide[s] swings

Power/lights: No

Shade: Some sheltered tables, man[y] trees

Swimming: Not recommended

Tables: Yes

Toilets: Yes

Water: Taps

Wheelchairs: Access limited to are[a] near entrance

Sydney history - Lane Cove

The area around Lane Cove National Park is rich in history. Before European settlement, small family groups of the Camaraigal clan, part of the Guringai tribe, lived along the river and evidence of their past can still be found in grinding grooves, rock shelters, shell middens and precious stone engravings. Tragically, soon after the arrival of the First Fleet in 1788, most of the local population was decimated by smallpox.

Another couple of decades brought the arrival of timber logging gangs, felling the fine stands of blackbutt, blue gum and red mahogany that lined Lane Cove River. There are still some specimens of these trees remaining, especially in the area around Fiddens Wharf and further north towards Thornleigh. During this time, Lane Cove was a kind of Sydney underworld, with convicts, criminals and gangs all making their mark.

With the timber exhausted, farmers moved into the area, planting orchards and vineyards. River traffic serviced local residents, but by the early 1900s, the area was used more for public recreation than for agriculture.

In 1938, a weir was built across the river — the one that still exists today — so that the area upstream was not only safe from sharks, but was ideal for boating, canoeing and swimming. With the weir came the heyday of Lane Cove as a picnic destination, with Sydneysiders swarming there on weekends, and the construction of a network of bushwalking tracks, stone steps and pathways.

However, because the weir stops the tidal ebb and flow of the river, the ecology of the area is imbalanced and upstream of the weir, the riverbanks are infested by grasses and exotic weeds. Although National Parks sometimes talk about dismantling the weir, something which would help restore the native vegetation upstream, vocal opponents see the weir as an important part of this area's vibrant history.

37 Buffalo Creek Reserve

This large grassy area is broken up into a small central playing field, BBQ area and a family area with a well-equipped, shaded playground and a bicycle 'practice area'. The reserve is on the Great North Walk and is the point of access for a particularly well-preserved section of bush: Sugarloaf Hill. Walk just 200-300 metres along the track and you'll forget you're in Sydney. Watch out for mosquitoes as the whole place is fringed by mangrove swamps.

At a glance

Address: Pittwater Road, Hunters Hill

Map refs: G 313/C3, S 255/Q15, U 214/H3

Public transport: Bus 538

Parking: Unrestricted car park

Entry fee: None

Opening times: 24 hours

BBQs: Wood (provided)

Boating: No

Dogs: Leashed

Kiosk/café: No

Playground: Slides, climbing frame, swings, shaded; basketball hoop

Power/lights: No

Shade: Sheltered tables

Swimming: No

Tables: Yes

Toilets: Yes

Water: Tap by basketball hoop

Wheelchairs: Toilet, good access

38 Clarkes Point Reserve

At a glance

Address: Clarke Road, Woolwich

Map refs: G 314/F14, S 276/M6, U 215/F14

Public transport: Woolwich Ferry (800 m), buses 505, 538 and 539 stop on Woolwich Rd (400 m)

Parking: Unrestricted car park

Entry fee: None

Opening times: 24 hours

BBQs: Wood (wood provided)

Boating: No

Dogs: Leashed, one small area for off leash

Kiosk/café: No

Playground: No

Power/lights: No

Shade: Trees around picnic spots

Swimming: Not recommended

Tables: Yes

Toilets: Yes

Water: No

Wheelchairs: Good access

A couple of grassy areas fringed with trees, Clarkes Point is modest in size but is a very peaceful spot, as well as being close to a couple of Sydney's lesser known but interesting historical sites. Kellys Bush, a piece of remnant bushland 300 metres to the west, was the focus of a protracted preservation struggle and was saved thanks to the unlikely combination of local residents and the NSW Builders Labourer's Federation (BLF). Much closer to hand, the Woolwich Dock was a huge undertaking completed soon after Federation. It became a very important WWII dry dock and is set to become a public marina.

Clifton Gardens

Lower North Shore and Middle Harbour

Many visitors to Sydney never head to the north side of the harbour, except for the obligatory ferry ride to Manly. So they fail to appreciate that the best place to view the city and take in the sheer sweep of it is from these northern suburban shores. Many of the recreational reserves and parks on the Lower North Shore offer just such rewarding views, as well as being less busy than their city counterparts. In contrast the birdlife seems more exuberant and the bush considerably wilder. Balls Head in particular is an outpost of bushland amazingly close to the city centre.

This feeling of being able to get back to the bush — just kilometres from the city centre — is heightened around the shores of Middle Harbour. Harold Reid Reserve is just one of a string of bushland parks and reserves in the upper reaches that blend gently into Garigal National Park to the north. There are several beaches here. Just one makes it into this volume in its own right as a 'best' beach, but it's one of Sydney's gems: Balmoral.

View from Cremorne Reserve

39 Berry Island

The main picnic area here is the small, grassy neck of the isthmus that connects the North Shore to Berry 'Island'. Fascinating views extend west to the Shell oil refinery and east to naval wharves. However the draw of this small park is the 'island' itself. Covered in bush, a 20-minute walk threads around the periphery, and several signs chart the significance of the site to the Camaraigal people who lived here at the time of the arrival of the First Fleet. Also a short walk away is Badangi Reserve, another preserved area of bush with marked paths running through it.

At a glance

Address: Shirley Road, Wollstonecraft

Map refs: G 315/B12, S 277/B5, U 215/M12

Public transport: Wollstonecraft Station (500 m), bus 265 stops at the station

Parking: Unrestricted on Shirley Rd

Entry fee: None

Opening times: 24 hours

BBQs: No

Boating: No

Dogs: Off leash on lawned area

Kiosk/café: No

Playground: Swings, climbing frame, ropes, slides

Power/lights: No

Shade: Small number of trees in park area

Swimming: No

Tables: No

Toilets: Yes

Water: Bubbler by playground

Wheelchairs: Toilet; good access to lawned area

Just east of Berry Island, Balls Head also has the feel of pristine bush (although it was all but cleared in the 1930s), and as such is the closest patch of bushland to the city centre. The bridge, city and Darling Harbour all seem almost close enough to touch from the small grassy lookout at the point. The BBQs and tables are away from the views in the midst of the bush.

At a glance

Address: Balls Head Drive, Waverton

Map refs: G 315/D16, S 277/C8, U 215/P15

Public transport: Waverton Station (600 m), bus 265 stops at the station

Parking: Unrestricted area on Balls Head Drive

Entry fee: None

Opening times: 24 hours

BBQs: Electric (free)

Boating: No

Dogs: Leashed

Kiosk/café: Couple in Waverton

Playground: Swings

Power/lights: No

Shade: Plenty of trees

Swimming: No

Tables: Yes, several

Toilets: Yes

Water: Taps

Wheelchairs: Toilet; access to some areas

City from Harbour View walk

41 Bradfield Park

Sydney Harbour Bridge rests one foot on Bradfield Park, providing an intimate perspective of this engineering marvel that is probably only bettered by doing the Bridge Climb itself. Frequent wedding parties testify to the park's equally fine Opera House and city backdrop, though it is perhaps too close for the New Year's Eve festivities. Though poor in park facilities, these views, plus the proximity of the Olympic Pool, Luna Park and the Bridge (it's a 20 minute walk to the Pylon Lookout), make this wide sweep of grass a good base for a family day out.

At a glance

Address: Broughton Street, Kirribilli

Map refs: G 316/A16, S 277/K9, U 216/F16

Public transport: Milsons Point Station (200 m), Milsons Point Ferry, bus 269 stops near the wharf

Parking: Some unrestricted at bottom of Broughton, otherwise 2-4 hours metered

Entry fee: None

Opening times: 24 hours

BBQs: No

Boating: No

Dogs: Off leash

Kiosk/café: Local cafés in Kirribili & Milsons Point. Ripples (T 9929 7722), just below the pool, is quite upmarket but easily has the best views. Open daily, but closed 1100-1200

Playground: Swings

Power/lights: No

Shade: Few trees & under bridge

Swimming: North Sydney Olympic Pool (charge)

Tables: Yes, several

Toilets: Yes

Water: No

Wheelchairs: Toilet; easy access to some areas

Out and about — Luna Park

In 1903 Luna Park opened on Coney Island in the United States and was so successful that Luna Parks began to pop up all over the world. Australia's first was in St Kilda in 1912 but it was not until 1935 that Sydney's Luna Park first flashed its welcoming grin over Sydney Harbour. The park was redeveloped and reopened in 2004 at a cost of $80 million. Open daily, entrance is free, and you can then buy tickets to individual rides. Don't miss the view from the top of the ferris wheel. T 9033 7676, www.lunaparksydney.com.

The ferris wheel at Luna Park

Out and about – North Sydney Olympic Pool

North Sydney Olympic Pool is actually two pools – an outdoor and an indoor – and there is also a gym, sauna and spa area. There are none of the now common slides and play areas for children, but this is none-the-less a unique pool. Open daily, 0700-1900 at weekends, entry $5.10 (children $2.50), T 9955 2309.

Out and about — Pylon Lookout

While walking accross the Harbour Bridge it is well worth climbing the 200 steps to the top of the Pylon Lookout. The views are naturally superb and there are interesting displays on the history of the bridge. Open daily 1000-1700, $8.50, (children over 7 $3, under 7 free.). T 9240 1100, www.pylonlookout.com.au.

42 Blues Point (McMahons Point)

The moment you first see this place you understand why so many people flock here on New Year's Eve. This is the only place in Sydney where you can stand directly opposite the full arch of the Sydney Harbour Bridge, and it's so close it only just fits in a standard camera lens. The reserve itself has few facilities, but the lawns are well maintained and give the place the pleasant feel of an amphitheatre. Luna Park and the North Sydney Olympic Pool (see previous page) are a 20-minute walk away.

At a glance

Address: Blues Point Road, McMahons Point

Map refs: G 315/G16, S 277/G9, U 236/B1

Public transport: Milsons Point Station (1.2 km), McMahons Point Ferry, buses 265 and 269 stop at the wharf

Parking: 4 hour restriction on week days

Entry fee: None

Opening times: 24 hours

BBQs: None

Boating: No

Dogs: Off leash

Kiosk/café: Many along upper Blues Point Rd

Playground: Swings, climbing frame

Power/lights: No

Shade: None

Swimming: No

Tables: One

Toilets: Yes

Water: Bubbler

Wheelchairs: Toilet; easy access to reserve

View from Blues Point

43 Cremorne Reserve (Robertsons Point)

Cremorne Reserve is the narrow but surprisingly peaceful walkway that wraps around Cremorne Point. The views of the city and Opera House from the Point and lower west side make this walk extremely popular. The best places to stop and spread out the picnic blanket are the grassy areas between the pool and ferry wharf, though the playground and toilets are beyond the tarmac on bush-covered Robertsons Point. The last survivor of many pools built by early residents of Cremorne Point, McCallum Pool vies with North Sydney Olympic Pool for the most dramatic backdrop of any pool in the harbour.

At a glance

Address: Milson Road, Cremorne Point

Map refs: G 316/G16, S 278/A8, U 216/M15

Public transport: Cremorne Point Ferry, bus 225 stops at the wharf

Parking: 4 hours restriction on most of Cremorne Point

Entry fee: None

Opening times: 24 hours

BBQs: No

Boating: No

Dogs: Leashed

Kiosk/café: Kiosk at the ferry wharf, open daily to 1530

Playground: Swings, climbing frame at Robertsons Point

Power/lights: No

Shade: Plenty of trees

Swimming: McCallum Pool (free entry and open, in theory, 24 hours, but note that it is very narrow and shallow)

Tables: No, many seats

Toilets: Yes

Water: Bubbler by McCallum Pool

Wheelchairs: Toilet; sealed paths

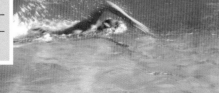

McCallum Pool

44 Ashton Park (Bradleys Head)

Part of Sydney Harbour National Park, Ashton Park comprises both open grassy areas and native bushland. The park is in close proximity to Taronga Zoo and the fascinating area of Bradleys Head. The latter i the site of the HMAS Sydney Memorial, 19th century gun emplacements, a small amphitheatre overlooking the vivid city views, and access to a small grassy foreshore and beach (often overlooked and a fine place to picnic and watch the yachts and ferries go by).

View across to the city from Bradleys Head

At a glance

Address: Bradleys Head Road, Mosman

Map refs: G 317/C16, S 278/G10, U 217/C16

Public transport: Taronga Zoo Ferry (800 m to main gate), bus 238 stops at the Zoo main entrance (800 m to main gate) and wharf

Parking: Car parks $3 per day, gates locked 2000; unrestricted (but busy) opposite Zoo main entrance

Entry fee: None

Opening times: 24 hours

BBQs: No

Boating: No

Dogs: No

Kiosk/café: Athol Hall (by entrance gate, T 9968 4441), open 1100-150C Tues-Fri & Sun (can be closed Apr-Aug), has only a handful of balcony tables but they do take lunch bookings

Playground: No

Power/lights: No

Shade: Plenty of trees, some shelters

Swimming: Small beach

Tables: No, many seats

Toilets: Yes

Water: No

Wheelchairs: Toilet; some sealed paths

Out and about — Taronga Zoo

Sydney's city centre zoo has been a much-loved fixture for some 90 years, and is still one of Sydney's most popular attractions, even opening on Christmas Day. Entrance is currently a not inconsiderable $32 (children under 15 $22.50), though this drops by over a quarter if you can muster a group of 12. For pre-bookings for groups T 9978 4782. A small saving can also be made by purchasing a joint ferry/entrance ticket at Circular Quay.

Sydney history — HMAS Sydney

The current *HMAS Sydney*, a guided missile frigate, is the fourth to carry the name, and has seen active service in both the 'Gulf' wars and in East Timor. It is about the same size as the first *HMAS Sydney*, a light cruiser that served in the First World War, sinking one enemy ship: the Emden. All four ships — and the men lost aboard them — are honoured at the memorial at Ashton Park, but the lion's share of fame and tragedy is taken by *HMAS Sydney II* which was sunk with all 645 hands while engaging and sinking the Kormoran during the Second World War. The mast and crow's nest on the point are from the first HMAS Sydney, not as many suppose, the second, which is thought to lie off the WA coast but has never been found.

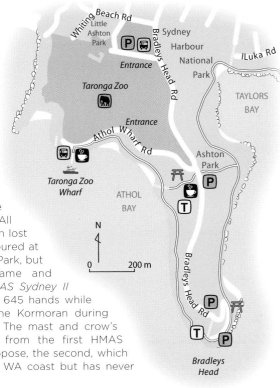

Sydney red gums on Athol Beach

45 Middle Head

Part of Sydney Harbour National Park, this large grassy area has grandstand views over North and South Heads and comes into its own for the start of the Sydney-Hobart yacht race every Boxing Day. The expansive vista is not, however, the only reward for choosing the out-of-the-way drive and short walk required. Children and adults alike find the extensive remains of the 19th century fort and gun emplacements fascinating, and they more than make up for any lack of playing area. There are guided tours of the fortifications and tunnels every fourth Sunday during Oct-May. Bookings are essential, call T 9247 5033.

At a glance

Address: Middle Head Road, Mosman

Map refs: G 317/K6, S 258/Q18, U 217/L6

Public transport: Bus 244 stops near Middle Head Oval (600 m), weekdays only

Parking: Unrestricted gravel area opposite the oval

Entry fee: None

Opening times: Gates locked 1700

BBQs: No

Boating: No

Dogs: No

Kiosk/café: No

Playground: No

Power/lights: No

Shade: None in picnic area

Swimming: At Obelisk Bay & Cobblers Beach (both nude beaches)

Tables: No

Toilets: Yes, by information centre

Water: Tap by the toilets

Wheelchairs: Reasonably good access

Gun emplacements at Middle Head

46 Clifton Gardens

This large grassy park is a popular summertime picnic area for families. The netted swimming area is a big draw, and increasingly so is the Harbour Trust area just to the east. Until recently a run-down, disused military site, the Trust is sprucing it up and leasing some buildings for various uses, including tea-rooms and artist studios. Tours of the fortifications are run every first Sunday in the month ($8, children $5, 8969 2131).

At a glance

Address: Morella Road, Mosman

Map refs: G 317/E12, S 278/J4, J 217/E12

Public transport: The 228 bus stops very near the entrance (Mon-Fri only); the next closest are the 233, 238 and 247

Parking: Expensive metered in car park, open 0700-2000; unrestricted on Morella Rd

Entry fee: None

Opening times: 24 hours

BBQs: No

Boating: No

Dogs: No

Kiosk/café: Bacino, just by entrance to military area

Playground: Basketball hoops; climbing frames

Power/lights: No

Shade: Small number of trees in park area

Swimming: Modest beach, partially netted; not patrolled

Tables: Many

Toilets: Yes

Water: Bubblers

Wheelchairs: Good access to grassy area

By far the most popular on the Lower North Shore, these two beaches are separated by the bridge to the tiny island of Rocky Point. Although there's a kilometre of beach here, it can still get very busy on a summer weekend. Families with younger children tend to congregate at the southern end. The water is usually relatively calm, making for excellent – and safe – swimming and snorkelling. Both ends of Edwards Beach are great for snorkelling. If you've ever fancied trying your hand at sailing, the friendly school at the southern end makes giving it a go very easy.

The Rotunda

At a glance

Address: The Esplanade, Balmoral

Map refs: G 317/E6, S 258/J17, U 217/E5

Public transport: Buses 233, 238 & 257

Parking: 1-4 hrs restricted (if you can find a spot) along the Esplanade; unrestricted on most side and back streets

Entry fee: None

Opening times: 24 hours

BBQs: For hire at Sailing School ($25), southern end of beaches

Boating: Kayaks, windsurfers and small sailing boats for hire at Sailing School from $15-50 per hour, open daily 0900-1700 (closed Mon-Tue in Winter), T 9960 5344, www.sailingschool.com.au

Dogs: Leashed on promenade

Kiosk/café: Several; the Bathers Pavilion Café (nr Rotunda, on foreshore) is recommended for an indulgent breakfast (open at 0700, queues from around 0800, no bookings), T 9969 5050. There is a kiosk near the playground at the southern end (also, see opposite)

Playground: Near southernmost pool; swings, various climbing frames

Power/lights: Street lighting

Shade: Many trees along the extensive foreshore

Showers: No

Snorkelling: Both ends of Edwards Beach

Surfing: No

Swimming: Three enclosed areas, beaches not patrolled

Tables: Several on the lawned areas

Toilets: Yes

Water: Occasional bubblers and taps

Wheelchairs: Toilets (southern end); paved esplanade continuous from southern pool to Bathers pavilion

The Bathers Pavilion

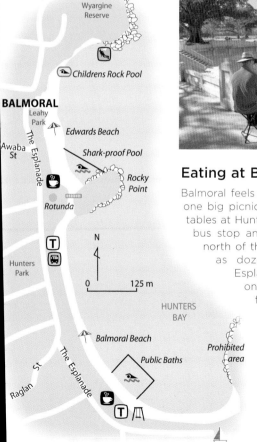

Wyargine
Reserve

Childrens Rock Pool

BALMORAL

Leahy
Park

Edwards Beach

Awaba
St

The Esplanade

Shark-proof Pool

Rocky
Point

Rotunda

Hunters
Park

N

0   125 m

HUNTERS
BAY

Balmoral Beach

Public Baths

Prohibited
area

Raglan St

The Esplanade

Eating at Balmoral

Balmoral feels like — and frequently is — one big picnic area. There are plenty of tables at Hunter Park, opposite the main bus stop and on the grassy area just north of the Bathers Pavilion, as well as dozens of seats along the Esplanade. The Bathers is just one of a range of eateries from kiosks to cafés to restaurants, mostly at the southern end of Balmoral. The Watermark (T 9968 3433) is very well regarded and also fronts directly onto the beach. Also at the southern end is Bottom of the Harbour, an excellent fish & chip and bottle shop.

48 Rosherville Reserve (Chinamans Beach)

The central tableau of weeping willows amidst an extensive lawn gives Rosherville Reserve a genteel atmosphere. The facilities are low-key and the beach screened by some bush-covered dunes, both helping to sustain the feel of an Edwardian country park. The disappointing playground is tucked away in a corner, so altogether Rosherville is a great destination to enjoy a little child-free space and time if that's what you're after.

At a glance

Address: McLean Crescent, Balmoral

Map refs: G 317/C1, S 258/H13, U 217/C1

Public transport: Bus 249 stops at the Medusa St lights (500 m)

Parking: Expensive ticketed area 0700-2000, but free and unrestricted in the road area adjacent

Entry fee: None

Opening times: 24 hours

BBQs: No

Boating: No

Dogs: Leashed 0900-1600 Sat-Sun, off leash otherwise

Kiosk/café: No

Playground: Swings, climbing frame

Power/lights: No

Shade: Some trees

Swimming: Chinamans Beach (harbour), not patrolled

Tables: No

Toilets: Yes

Water: Bubbler by toilets

Wheelchairs: Reasonably good access

49 Harold Reid Reserve

Harold Reid Reserve is an extensive area of bush on two distinct levels, with a stunning walking track threading through the lower, foreshore area and a loop road providing access to the higher ground, where the picnic area is. The picnic area doubles as the car park (not sealed), but since this is a relatively quiet picnic area this usually isn't a problem. There are no views from the picnic area, but a short stroll away is a lookout with extensive views over Middle Harbour.

At a glance

Address: Rembrandt Drive, Middle Cove

Map refs: G 286/C8, S 257/N5, U 196/H8

Bookings: No

Public transport: Bus 275 circles Rembrandt Dr (not Sun); buses 205-210 stop on Eastern Valley Way (1 km)

Parking: Unrestricted car park, gates locked 1730

Entry fee: None

Opening times: 24 hours

BBQs: Gas (free)

Boating: No

Dogs: Leashed

Kiosk/café: No

Playground: No

Power/lights: No

Shade: Many trees

Swimming: No

Tables: Yes

Toilets: Yes

Water: Bubbler

Wheelchairs: Reasonably good access

View over Castle Cove

50 Davidson Park

Part of the Garigal National Park, Davidson sits in a small valley hugging the lower reaches of Middle Harbour Creek. Despite being almost in the shadow of Roseville Bridge there is little road noise, making this one of the most peaceful places in the lower North Shore. The picnic areas are long and grassy with many trees providing lots of shade. A major feature of the park is the bushtrack that heads off along the river/harbour for several kilometres in both directions. Note that you need to be travelling south to take the turn to the access road.

At a glance

Address: Warringah Road, Forestville

Map refs: G 255/G14, S 237/G14, U 176/B14

Public transport: None close. The 136, 137 and L60 buses stop in Roseville and Forestville (both about a 2 km walk)

Parking: Unrestricted car park, closes 1800 (2000 daylight saving)

Entry fee: $7 per car (or free with NPWS pass)

Opening times: 24 hours

Bookings: One gas BBQ area and adjacent tables can be booked

BBQs: A few gas (free); many wood (wood provided)

Boating: Boat ramp

Dogs: No

Kiosk/café: No

Playground: No

Power/lights: No

Shade: Plenty of trees

Swimming: Netted area in the river

Tables: Many

Toilets: Yes

Water: Taps

Wheelchairs: Toilets; good access

51 Clontarf Reserve

This very popular reserve has a range of facilities that make it ideal for families with young children and it is always buzzing on a summer weekend. The sprawling lawned area is largely shaded by trees, there are three sets of BBQs, a large and varied playground, a shallow, netted swimming area and a peaceful outlook over to the yacht clubs on the spit. It's also near the Spit end of the Spit-to-Manly walk and there are picturesque paths in either direction, particularly toward Grotto Point (allow two hours return).

Storm Boy rides again!

At a glance

Address: Bay Road, Clontarf

Map refs: G 287/E14, S 258/J10, U 197/E14

Public transport: Buses 132 & 171 stop on Beatrice St (400 m)

Parking: Expensive ticketed area 0800-1800, but free and unrestricted on adjacent roads

Entry fee: None

Opening times: 24 hours

BBQs: Electric (free)

Boating: No

Dogs: No

Kiosk/café: Clonny's (T 9948 2373) kiosk (0930-1630) and café (1200-1630 if no function) open daily

Playground: Large and shaded; swings, slides, several climbing frames

Power/lights: Lights

Shade: Many trees, some sheltered tables

Swimming: Shark-proof area

Tables: Many

Toilets: Yes

Water: Taps

Wheelchairs: Toilets; good access

This charming spot is more often accessed by water than by land; the bay is a popular mooring spot for those in search of a quiet lunch. This tiny area of grass, surrounded by bush, sits on the foreshore opposite the Magazine Complex in Bantry Bay. Foot access is from Seaforth Oval: look for the Garigal National Park sign on the right of the roadside bus turning area, then follow the Timber Getters track quite steeply downhill for about 20 minutes. Beyond the picnic spot the track continues along the foreshore and into the heart of this area of the Park.

At a glance

Address: Wakehurst Parkway, Seaforth

Map refs: G 286/H2, S 238/B17, U 196/M2

Public transport: Buses 169, 172 & 173 stop near Seaforth Oval (1 km)

Parking: Unrestricted car park by the oval

Entry fee: None

Opening times: 24 hours

BBQs: Wood (bring your own)

Boating: Jetty, no launching

Dogs: No

Kiosk/café: No

Playground: No

Shade: Many trees

Swimming: Not recommended

Tables: Yes

Toilets: Yes

Water: No

Wheelchairs: No

Bantry Bay: the picnic spot is just left of the yachts

53 Manly Dam

Manly Warringah War Memorial Park covers 377 hectares of native bushland and includes the largest freshwater lake in Sydney, with open grassy picnic areas stretching along the southern shore. There's a couple of small beaches, heaps of shade and lots of BBQs and picnic spots. They can get very busy, however, and booking is recommended for large groups. Surrounding the dam is an 11-kilometre mountain bike circuit of medium technical difficulty, as well as a network of bushwalking tracks. Waterskiing is allowed, phone 9451 8880 at least a week prior to organise permission.

At a glance

Address: King Street, Manly Vale

Map refs: G 287/E3, S 238/J19, U 197/F3

Bookings: Tables can be booked, 9942 2545 (charges apply)

Public transport: Bus 145 (weekdays only), otherwise one of the many that stop on Condamine St nr King St (900 metres)

Parking: Unrestricted, but closed from around dusk to 0700

Entry fee: Vehicle charge ($7) on Sundays & public holidays

Opening times: 24 hours

BBQs: 2 electric (free) plus many woodfired (wood provided)

Boating: Yes, boat ramp

Dogs: On walking tracks only

Kiosk/café: No

Playground: Swings, slides and climbing frame

Power/lights: No

Shade: Many trees, some shelters

Swimming: Yes, in the dam

Tables: Yes, several

Toilets: Yes

Water: Taps & bubblers

Wheelchairs: Toilets; good access

Turimetta Beach

Northern Beaches & Ku-ring-gai

Between Manly and Barrenjoey Head, along some 30 kilometres of coast, are nearly 20 distinct beaches, with several more in North Harbour and Pittwater. Picking a handful from these is no easy task, and no doubt there will be howls of protest from several readers of this book about our choices! The beaches range from the very small to one of nearly four kilometres in length, and offer a wide range of facilities and degrees of access. Most are patrolled and almost all have good surfing conditions at least part of the time.

Most of these beaches are enclosed at either end by lofty headlands, many of which are undeveloped and protected as reserves. Some headlands are still bush-covered, others have grassy areas for exercising and picnicking. The views from Mona Vale headland are particularly fine and not to be missed.

Ku-ring-gai Chase National Park is one of the largest in the Sydney region. It gets its name from the Guringai Aboriginal people, the original inhabitants of the land to the north of Sydney harbour. The park is a very special place, with not only one of the greatest concentrations of rock art in the world, but 15,000 hectares of rugged sandstone bushland and an enormous diversity of birds, mammals and wildflowers.

Barrenjoey Head from West Head

54 North Harbour Reserve & beaches

Unlike Port Jackson and Middle Harbour, North Harbour ends abruptly, with no long inlets and creeks like its southern neighbours. Virtually the entire shoreline, a mix of small picturesque beaches, bush, grassy areas and suburban development, is accessible via the eastern part of the Spit-to-Manly walk, and many of these spots make for a great picnic, including North Harbour Reserve which has the most facilities. In the middle, Fairlight Beach is one of the best snorkelling spots in Sydney, and you're likely to see octopuses, anenomes and schools of fish.

At a glance

Address: (North Harbour Reserve): Condamine Street, Balgowlah

Map refs: (North Harbour Reserve): G 287/K10, S 258/P6, U 197/K10

Public transport: Manly Ferry (1 km from Fairlight Beach), buses 131 and 132

Parking: Unrestricted in nearby streets

Entry fee: None

Opening times: 24 hours

BBQs: Electric (free)

Boating: No

Dogs: Leashed

Kiosk/café: Shop at the Park, next to the reserve, sells a modest range of takeaway drinks and snacks

Playground: Slides, swings, climbing frames; basketball hoop at the reserve

Power/lights: No

Shade: A few trees, sheltered table

Snorkelling: Excellent, Pro Dive run snorkelling tours, T 1800 820 520

Swimming: Harbour pools at Forty Baskets & Fairlight beaches

Tables: Some, a couple shaded

Toilets: Yes, at the reserve

Water: No

Wheelchairs: Good access

Shelly is by far the most sheltered of the two beaches flanking Manly Beach and usually suitable for swimming even if the sea is quite rough. Although not very broad it extends back some distance toward its small grassy reserve, making for a surprising amount of towel room. The beach and reserve sit in a steep-sided cove, inaccessible to passing traffic, with both a laid-back café and well-regarded restaurant right by the sand. All this, plus a little patch of bush on the headland, make it a favourite of locals and visitors.

At a glance

Address: Bower Street, Manly

Map refs: G 289/B11, S 259/K7, J 198/G11; also see overleaf

Public transport: Manly Ferry (1.2 km), bus 135 stops in Bower St – several buses services terminate in Manly

Parking: Restricted (and expensive) car park 0800-1800, unrestricted on the local part of Bower St

Entry fee: None

Opening times: 24 hours

BBQs: Electric (free)

Boating: No

Dogs: Leashed in upper reserve

Kiosk/café: Sandbar café and Le Kiosk restaurant (T9977 4122, restaurant open daily, lunch from 1200, dinner from 1830; café 0900 to at least 1600, closes when wet)

Playground: No

Power/lights: Some street lighting

Shade: A few trees

Showers: Yes

Snorkelling: Yes, lots of butterfly fish under rocky ledges

Surfing: No

Swimming: Ocean (sheltered), not patrolled; also some rock baths halfway along the path to Manly Beach

Tables: Yes

Toilets: Yes

Water: Bubblers

Wheelchairs: Toilet, good access

56 Manly and North Steyne Beaches

Manly is Sydney's 'other' famous ocean beach and, thanks to the enjoyable long ferry ride, probably gets as many (if not more) visitors than Bondi. Despite being over 1.5 kilometres long, it can often be heaving with locals and day-trippers, families and teens, picnickers and diners, sports nuts and sun junkies, driving the crowd-shy around the far ends to either Shelly or Freshwater. Even when there's a crush, however, this is a very friendly spot, with no pretensions, and closer in spirit to Coogee than Bondi. It's also very child-friendly, with a great local aquarium and the opportunity to learn surfing or beach volleyball. The beach next to the wharf is a calm harbour beach, suitable for small children or those who don't like surf.

At a glance

Address: North Steyne/South Steyne, Manly

Map refs: G 288/H8, S 259/F5, U 198/C8

Public transport: Manly Ferry (400 m), Manly bus terminal (300 m) Parking: All nearby streets restricted to 2 hrs, some metered

Entry fee: None

Opening times: 24 hours

BBQs: No

Boating: No

Dogs: Leashed on promenade

Kiosk/café: Many on South/North Steyne and at the wharf; the Ocean Beach Café being the only actual beachside option (T 9977 0566); there's a small kiosk at the Manly LSC at the southern end

Playground: Slides, climbing frames – see opposite for details of other activities

Power/lights: Street lighting on foreshore

Shade: Tree-lined foreshore, some sheltered seating and tables

Showers: Yes, but well spaced out

Snorkelling: No

Surfing: Yes

Swimming: Ocean, patrolled; rock baths at northern end and just beyond southern end

Tables: Yes, along foreshore

Toilets: Yes

Water: Bubblers/taps

Wheelchairs: Toilets at Manly SLC & Ocean Beach Café, paved esplanade

Out and about – Oceanworld

Located on the West Esplanade on Manly's small harbour beach, Oceanworld is well worth a diversion from the ocean beach. The main tank is a generous 5,000,000 litres, quite big enough to be the home to several grey nurse sharks, rays, turtles and plenty of fish. Rather excitingly, you can go for a short dive in this tank. Experienced divers have been known to emerge from the experience grinning from ear to ear, and since it requires no dive accreditation or previous experience it can make for an excellent introduction to scuba. Open daily 1000-1730, admission $17.95, children $9.50, shark dives from $245 (www.oceanworld.com.au, T 8251 7877).

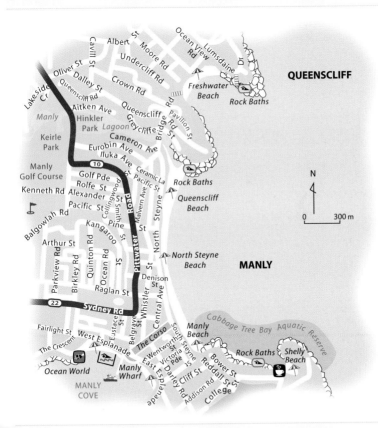

Out and about – surfing and beach volleyball

Take your pick: two well-run sporting schools can be found at Manly. The Manly Surf School offers lessons to various groups including adults-only and children-only. The price depends on how long you commit for, and can be as low as $33 per lesson for 10 lessons (for details see www.manlysurfschool.com, T 9977 6977). The people at Beach Volleyball also offer a range of short courses and one-off lessons, from $30. There is usually a Saturday class (for details see www.beachvolleyball.com.au, T 1300 865 539).

Freshwater Beach is in Queenscliff Bay in the suburb of Harbord, but despite the odd nomenclature this is a peach of a spot, much loved by locals. It may only be 300 metres long, but it stretches back a good 100 metres to the dunes, so there's a lot of sand here. Tightly enclosed by headlands, Freshwater has a surprisingly private feel, and the lack of commercialism — in stark contrast to the beach's immediate neighbour, Manly — makes it feel quite off the beaten track. It's also one of smallest beaches to have its own rock baths, a bonus for families when the sea is a bit rough for kids.

At a glance

Address: Kooloora Avenue, Harbord

Map refs: G 288/J2, S 239/G18, U 198/D2; and see map on previous page

Public transport: Buses E65 and 139 stop in Charles St

Parking: Metered car park, unrestricted on nearby streets

Entry fee: None

Opening times: 24 hours

BBQs: Electric (free) in reserve

Boating: No

Dogs: Leashed in reserve

Kiosk/café: Dukes, open seasonally and according to weather, daily in summer school holidays

Playground: Slides, swings in reserve

Power/lights: No

Shade: Sheltered tables in reserve

Showers: Yes

Snorkelling: Yes, on a calm day

Surfing: Yes

Swimming: Ocean, patrolled; rock baths at northern end

Tables: Yes in reserve

Toilets: Yes

Water: No

Wheelchairs: Access to reserve

Walking the Northern Beaches

areel Head from Bangalley Head

It is possible to walk the entire 30 kilometres from Palm Beach to Manly along the beaches and clifftops. The route is a string of long golden surf beaches, linked by headlands with wonderful views. Naturally, all the coastal real estate is highly prized so you are never far from a multi-million dollar home! There are short road sections, but many of the beaches of the Upper North Shore are enclosed by cliffs or dunes and feel somehow private and untamed in comparison to the busy Eastern suburbs beaches. Much of the route from Palm Beach right through to Manly is detailed in one of the companion books to this one: *Sydney's Best Harbour & Coastal Walks*.

w from Long Reef.

58 Dee Why Beach

Having recently undergone a smart foreshore makeover, long Dee Why neatly offers both a chic, suburban beach experience and, towards its far northern end, a considerably more peaceful and out of the way one. Much of the beach backs onto the broad sweep of Dee Why Lagoon, which completely cuts out any hint of noise from Pittwater Road, and to the north is the thrusting headland of Long Reef. North of Dee Why surf club is 'No Man's Land', an area where dangerous rips dominate, sometimes running out to sea like rivers. As always swimmers should stay between the flags. .

At a glance

Address: The Strand, Dee Why

Map refs: G 259/A6, S 239/J5, U 178/F6

Public transport: Many buses stop in Dee Why on the Pittwater Rd (600 m)

Parking: Metered car park, unrestricted in most nearby streets

Entry fee: None

Opening times: 24 hours

BBQs: No

Boating: No

Dogs: Leashed on foreshore

Kiosk/café: Several on The Strand

Playground: Slides, swings, climbing frame

Power/lights: Street lights

Shade: A few trees on southern foreshore

Showers: Yes

Snorkelling: Yes, at southern end

Surfing: Yes

Swimming: Ocean, patrolled; rock baths at southern end

Tables: Yes

Toilets: Yes

Water: Taps in toilets

Wheelchairs: Toilets, good access t foreshore

59 Fishermans Beach

The southern end of Fishermans can be a little scruffy but it's the only stretch of sheltered beach for miles, making it good for a calm swim, particularly when there's a southerly blowing. It's part of an aquatic reserve, so snorkelling can be quite rewarding too. With headlands at either end the beach would have quite a secluded feel but for the golf club bistro garden and Long Reef access road. From the southern end it's a short and very pleasant walk up to superb views at the top of Long Reef headland.

At a glance

Address: Anzac Avenue, Collaroy

Map refs: G 229/E15, S 219/N19, M 158/K15

Public transport: Many buses services stop in Collaroy on the Pittwater Rd (800 m)

Parking: Metered car park 0700-1900, unrestricted in nearby streets

Entry fee: None

Opening times: 24 hours

BBQs: No

Boating: No

Dogs: Leashed on foreshore

Kiosk/café: No

Playground: No

Power/lights: No

Shade: No

Showers: No

Snorkelling: Yes, at southern end

Surfing: No

Swimming: Ocean, sheltered

Tables: No

Toilets: Yes

Water: No

Wheelchairs: Not good access

60 Collaroy Beach

Collaroy is at the southern end of the longest uninterrupted stretch of sand in either the northern beaches or the eastern suburbs, nearly 4 kilometres in all. Most of the facilities, including rock baths and a patrolled swimming area, are found at this southern end. From here, it's only a short walk to Fisherman's Beach (see page 93) and on to Long Reef headland. The picnic facilities are on the reserve areas either side of the block that contains the Surf Rock Hotel.

At a glance

Address: Birdwood Avenue, Collaroy

Map refs: G 229/C12, S 219/L16, U 158/H12

Public transport: Many buses services stop in Collaroy on the Pittwater Rd (200 m)

Parking: Unrestricted on local streets, several metered car parks

Entry fee: None

Opening times: 24 hours

BBQs: Electric (free)

Boating: No

Dogs: Leashed on foreshore reserve

Kiosk/café: The Deck (part of the Surf Rock Hotel) is right on the beach, open long hours daily

Playground: Slides, swings, climbing frames; shaded

Power/lights: Street lights in reserve

Shade: A few trees

Showers: Yes

Snorkelling: No

Surfing: Yes, good for beginners

Swimming: Ocean, patrolled; rock baths

Tables: Yes

Toilets: Yes

Water: Taps

Wheelchairs: Toilet, foreshore access

Just inland from Narrabeen Beach, there are several picnic spots on the shores of the major Narrabeen Lake. On the northern side, the Billarong Sanctuary and Middle Creek Reserve do get a lot of road noise from the Wakehurst Parkway, but Billarong is otherwise a very pleasant spot. On the southern side Jamieson Park is large and mostly bush, but with a few secluded grassy areas, each with a wood BBQ. Wheeler Park is very small but has a very good playground, and is a short walk from the well-situated Blowfish Café.

At a glance

Address (Jamieson Park): The Esplanade, Narrabeen

Map refs (Jamieson Park): S 228/G6, S 219/E10, U 158/B6

Public transport: Many buses services stop in Narrabeen on the Pittwater Rd (1 km from Jamieson)

Parking: Metered car parks, unrestricted in nearby streets

Entry fee: None

Opening times: 24 hours

BBQs: Electric (free); wood in the grassy areas at Jamieson

Boating: Boat ramps (not at Wheeler); kayak hire at Jamieson (T 9960 5899, www.kayakadventuresports.com.au)

Dogs: Leashed

Kiosk/café: Blowfish Café in Narrabeen St (nr Wheeler), open daily for breakfast and lunch, T 9913 8938

Playground (Wheeler): Slides, swings, climbing frames

Power/lights: No

Shade: Trees in all locations

Swimming: Lake

Tables: Yes

Toilets: Yes

Water: Bubblers/taps

Wheelchairs: Generally good access

62 Turimetta Beach

Of all Sydney's large suburban beaches, Turimetta is probably the most natural, serene and beautiful. A couple of houses are visible from the beach but the high surrounding cliffs, untamed vegetation and complete absence of road access and shore-side buildings really does make you feel like you could be hundreds of kilometres north of the city. At high tide, the water reaches to the cliff face, so there's no beach at all. At low tide, the rock ledge leading as far as Narabeen becomes accessible, exposing many Aboriginal engravings.

At a glance

Address: Park Parade, Warriewood

Map refs: G 199/E14, S 219/N2, U 138/K14

Public transport: The 155 bus heads down Sydney Rd, otherwise several stop on Pittwater Rd (600 m) in Warriewood

Parking: Unrestricted on nearby streets

Entry fee: None

Opening times: 24 hours

BBQs: None

Boating: No

Dogs: No

Kiosk/café: No

Playground: No

Power/lights: No

Shade: No

Showers: No

Snorkelling: Yes

Surfing: Yes, strong shore break

Swimming: Ocean, not patrolled, rock baths via Peal Place

Tables: No

Toilets: No

Water: Taps in reserve

Wheelchairs: No

63 Mona Vale headland

Widely regarded as having the best view in the Northern Beaches and thus one of the best in Sydney, from this high headland you can see from the tip of the Central Coast right down to Manly. There are no facilities, it's a very small area and not a great place to picnic if there's a stiff breeze blowing, but this is nevertheless one of the must-see destinations in this section. The immediate southern view takes in Basin and Mona Vale beaches with their unusual rock pool. Best access to the beaches is via Surfview Road.

At a glance

Address: Hillcrest Avenue, Mona Vale

Map refs: G 199/J3, S 200/A11, U 138/P3

Public transport: The E84 bus heads down Surfview Rd, otherwise several services stop on Barrenjoey Rd

Parking: Unrestricted in Hillcrest Ave

Entry fee: None

Opening times: 24 hours

BBQs: No

Boating: No

Dogs: Leashed

Kiosk/café: No

Playground: No

Power/lights: No

Shade: No

Swimming: No

Tables: Some seats

Toilets: No

Water: Taps

Wheelchairs: Good access

Looking south over Basin and Mona Vale beaches

64 Bungan Beach

Ringed by high cliffs, Bungan doesn't have very easy access. A kind-hearted driver might drop you at the bottom of the single (steep) access road, but otherwise it's one of two long steep walks, the one down Beach Road being the shortest (there is no vehicular access down this road except for residents). This, plus only basic facilities, make this very much a locals' beach and so usually uncrowded.

At a glance

Address: Bungan Head or Beach Roads, Newport

Map refs: G 169/J15, S 200/A7, U 118/P15

Public transport: Several Services stop at Newport on Barrenjoey Rd (600 m)

Parking: Unrestricted in nearby streets (no parking or turning on Beach Road which is basically for residents access only)

Entry fee: None

Opening times: 24 hours

BBQs: No

Boating: No

Dogs: No

Kiosk/café: No

Playground: No

Power/lights: No

Shade: No

Showers: Yes

Snorkelling: No

Surfing: Yes

Swimming: Ocean, patrolled (Dec/Jan), beware of strong rips

Tables: No

Toilets: Yes

Water: Taps in toilets

Wheelchairs: Very limited access

Though similar in feel to Bungan, Bilgola has much better access. It also has more facilities and a splendid little kiosk overlooking the beach. You have to park in one of the car parks (there's an overspill section on the far side of the access road) so make sure you take sufficient change. On your drive out (or in) it's well worth stopping off at the A.J. Small Lookout at Bilgola Head, for some of the finest views in Sydney.

At a glance

Address: The Serpentine, Bilgola Beach

Map refs: G 170/B6, S 180/D18, J 119/B6

Public transport: A handful of buses (particularly the L90) stop on Barrenjoey Rd near the end of The Serpentine

Parking: Metered 0600-2100 - $1.50 $1 for each hour

Entry fee: None

Opening times: 24 hours

BBQs: No

Boating: No

Dogs: No

Kiosk/café: Open long hours during daylight – may also open some evenings in summer

Playground: No

Power/lights: No

Shade: No

Showers: Yes

Snorkelling: No

Surfing: Yes

Swimming: Ocean, patrolled; rock baths, treacherous rip at southern end

Tables: No

Toilets: Yes

Water: Taps

Wheelchairs: Not good access

66 Bangalley Head

A long, well-kept lawn separates the cliff edge of the lower southern slopes of Bangalley Head from the back gardens of several very well-situated houses. There are no facilities here, and no long sweeping views, but it is nevertheless a very picturesque and peaceful spot and if you're feeling energetic you can take the 250-odd uneven steps through the bush up to the top of the headland to take in the views from there. Access is via an easily missed track (marked Marine Road on the UBD and Gregory's) on Marine Parade just to the south of the junction with Watkins Road.

At a glance

Address: Marine Parade, North Avalon

Map refs: G 140/F14, S 180/H10, U 99/F14

Public transport: The local 193 bus heads down Marine Pde, and a handful of services stop nearby on Barrenjoey Rd

Parking: Unrestricted on Marine Pde

Entry fee: None

Opening times: 24 hours

BBQs: No

Boating: No

Dogs: No

Kiosk/café: No

Playground: No

Power/lights: No

Shade: Only on the track up to the headland

Swimming: No

Tables: There are a couple of seats

Toilets: No

Water: No

Wheelchairs: Access to picnic area

One of the very best all-round beaches in Sydney, Whale Beach is large enough to never feel too crowded and boasts just about every facility you might need. The BBQs are wood (and in some disrepair) rather than gas or electric, and the restaurant/kiosk isn't right on the beach, but other than that it's very difficult to find fault. If you are prepared to walk a little way there's even unrestricted parking in nearby streets.

At a glance

Address: The Strand, Whale Beach

Map refs: G 140/C6, S 180/E2, J 99/C6

Public transport: The local 193 bus heads down Whale Beach Rd, and a handful of services stop on Barrenjoey Rd

Parking: Metered 0600-2100 - $1.50 - $1 per hour; unrestricted in nearby streets

Entry fee: None

Opening times: 24 hours

BBQs: Wood (provided if you're lucky)

Boating: No

Dogs: No

Kiosk/café: Whale Beach Restaurant & Kiosk (T 9974 4009)

Playground: Swings, climbing frames

Power/lights: No

Shade: Norfolk Island pines on the grassy foreshore

Showers: Yes

Snorkelling: No

Surfing: Yes

Swimming: Ocean, patrolled; rock baths

Tables: Yes

Toilets: Yes

Water: Taps

Wheelchairs: Toilet, access to grassy foreshore

68 Palm Beach

The imposing hammerhead of Barrenjoey Head looks down on one of northern Sydney's favourite and best-known beaches: Palm Beach (or 'Summer Bay' if you're a Home & Away fan). This long beach is on the eastern, ocean side of the long, sandy isthmus that connects the headland to the rest of the Avalon peninsula. On the western side is Station (also known as Barrenjoey) Beach and between them is a long grassy reserve with various facilities. The walk up to the lighthouse on the headland is not as exacting as it looks and is a very rewarding expedition

At a glance

Address: Beach Road, Palm Beach

Map refs: G 109/K14, S 160/B14, U 78/Q14

Public transport: The L90 and 190 terminate at Ocean Pl

Parking: Metered from 0600-2100 in car park and in local streets

Entry fee: None

Opening times: 24 hours

BBQs: Electric (free) in reserve

Boating: For hire from Barrenjoey Boating Services at the seaplane wharf, T 9974 4229

Dogs: Leashed in reserve area

Kiosk/café: Carmels by the Sea at the seaplane wharf, Mon-Fri 0900-1700; Sat-Sun 0800-1700 (T 9974 4374)

Playground: Slides, swings, climbing frames in the reserve

Power/lights: No

Shade: Many trees in reserve and on foreshore

Showers: At south end by toilets

Snorkelling: Off Station Beach

Surfing: Yes

Swimming: Ocean (patrolled); harbour (Station Beach); rock baths

Tables: Yes, in reserve

Toilets: Yes, in reserve and at southern end of Palm

Water: No

Wheelchairs: Access to some areas

Southern end of Palm Beach

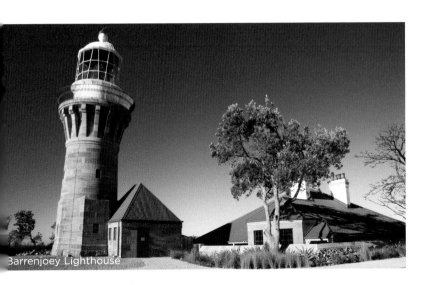
Barrenjoey Lighthouse

Sydney History — Barrenjoey Lighthouse

Barrenjoey Head was named by Governor Arthur Phillip during a survey of the area in 1788 and is thought to mean little kangaroo or wallaby. This landmark served an increasingly busy shipping route by the 1850s when the first light, just a fire in a basket in rough weather, was established here. The permanent lighthouse was built in 1881 from Hawkesbury sandstone quarried on site. At an elevation of 113 m, the light can be seen from 40 kilometres away and is equivalent to the light from the headlights of 75 cars. The NPWS completed a five-year restoration of the site in 2005 and the lighthouse is now open for tours on Sundays, every half hour from 1100 to 1500. Meet at the keeper's cottage on top. Adults $3, children $2. Bookings not required. For more information T 9472 9300 or www.nationalparks.nsw.gov.au.

(map labels) Barrenjoey Head Aquatic Reserve, Shark Point, Ku-ring-gai Chase National Park, Barrenjoey Lighthouse, PITTWATER, Recreation Reserve, Station Beach, Barrenjoey Head, TASMAN SEA, Boat Hire, Sea Plane Jetty, Palm Beach, Governor Phillip Park, Palm Beach Golf Course, North Palm Beach SLSC, Beach Rd, Warriewood Rd, Northview Rd, Sunrise Rd, Ocean Rd, Florida Rd, Palm Beach Rd, Barrenjoey Rd, 300 m, N

69 Clareville Beach & Picnic Area

Clareville doesn't particularly impress at first glance but is a perennial favourite of local families. The relatively thin strip of sand is overlooked by a large moored fleet of yachts, and the grassy foreshore is modest compared to others in the area. However, the swimming and paddling is very safe for children, and the BBQ and picnic area, right on the beach, is excellent. This beach is usually busy, so come early to bag your spot.

At a glance

Address: Delecta Avenue, Clareville

Map refs: G 169/F1, S 179/P13, U 118/L1

Public transport: Buses E89, 191 and 192 all stop very close by

Parking: Metered 0600-2100 - $1.50 + $1 per hour; unrestricted in nearby streets

Entry fee: None

Opening times: 24 hours

BBQs: Electric (free)

Boating: Sand boat ramp

Dogs: No

Kiosk/café: No

Playground: No

Power/lights: Street lighting in picnic area

Shade: A few trees

Showers: Yes

Snorkelling: Yes, at southern end

Surfing: No

Swimming: Harbour, netted pool at western end

Tables: Yes

Toilets: Yes

Water: Taps in toilets

Wheelchairs: Toilet, good access to picnic area

This small park is tucked away in a notch in the winding foreshore of Pittwater. Manicured lawns and modest facilities overlook Salt Pan Cove. This is a simple park for simple pleasures, but one of the best-kept and well-situated of its kind. Even better, the park is often deserted, even on days when the local beaches are heaving.

At a glance

Address: Prince Alfred Parade, Bilgola Plateau

Map refs: G 169/D7, S 179/M19, U 118/J7

Public transport: None close

Parking: Unrestricted

Entry fee: None

Opening times: 24 hours

BBQs: No

Boating: No

Dogs: Leashed

Kiosk/café: No

Playground: Swings, climbing frames

Power/lights: No

Shade: A few trees

Swimming: No

Tables: Yes

Toilets: Yes

Water: Bubbler

Wheelchairs: Good access

Very much a family park, the children's play area here is large with lots of equipment and is very clean and well shaded. The well-regarded Flying Fox café, right by the play area, is a modern affair with most of the usual light meal options. Offering a clear view of Newport and out into Pittwater, this is a very civilized place for a kids' party or a family BBQ, and the large wide open grass areas are ideal for ball games.

At a glance

Address: Mona Street, Mona Vale

Map refs: G 169/C15, S 199/L7, U 118/H15

Public transport: Buses E86, 155 and 156 all stop very close by

Parking: Unrestricted in nearby streets

Entry fee: None

Opening times: 24 hours

BBQs: Gas (free)

Boating: Ramps in nearby Bayview Park

Dogs: Leashed

Kiosk/café: Flying Fox Café, open 0800-1630 Mon-Weds, 0800-2100 Thurs-Sat, 0800-1800 Sun (T 9986 0980)

Playground: Slides, swings, climbing frames and flying fox

Power/lights: No

Shade: A few trees, sheltered tables

Swimming: Creek and harbour

Tables: Yes

Toilets: Yes, by the café

Water: Bubblers

Wheelchairs: Good access

72 Scotland Island

Leafy Scotland Island can be visited by ferry from Church Point, ferries leaving once an hour. The best picnic spot is at Catherine Park, next to the Tennis Court wharf. This is a fairly simple spot but just being on this car-free island surrounded by bushland and ocean (albeit with lots of boats and some houses in the scene) provides a certain sense of adventure. You can also walk to the top of the island where there's another small park. Alternatively you can walk right round the island, a circuit that takes about 40 minutes.

At a glance

Address: Pittwater

Map refs: G 168/H4, S 179/F15, J 118/B2

Public transport: Church Point Ferry (T 9999 3492) runs every hour on the half hour at weekends, check times for weekdays ($12.40 adults/$6.40 concession & kids/free for under fives); Buses E86, 155 and 156 all stop at Church Point

Parking: Some metered, some unrestricted parking at Church Point

Entry fee: None

Opening times: 24 hours

BBQs: No

Boating: Wharf

Dogs: Leashed

Kiosk/café: No

Playground: Slides, swings, climbing frame

Power/lights: No

Shade: Many trees

Swimming: Harbour

Tables: Yes

Toilets: Yes

Water: No

Wheelchairs: Difficult access, steep paths

Ku-ring-gai Chase National Park

With the arrival of the First Fleet, the life of the Guringai people changed forever, as settlers cleared the land of hardwood timbers, in particular red cedar, blue gum and blackbutt. However, in 1894 Ku-ring-gai was declared a national park and since that time the tall timbers have slowly regenerated. Today, the land feels surprisingly remote with steep-sided river valleys, kilometres of coastline, sheltered creeks and tidal mangroves.

Ku-ring-gai has one of the highest concentrations of rock art in the world. Rock engravings are generally found in groups, with figures ranging from several to over one hundred in number. Figures include fish, whales (some up to eight metres long), wallabies and mythical beings. Three of the most accessible rock art sites are The Basin Track, Echidna Aboriginal site (which has disabled access) and the Aboriginal Heritage Walk, which circuits from Resolute Picnic Area down to Red Hands Cave, and then back via Resolute Beach and West Head Beach.

There is an extensive network of other walking tracks throughout the park, from short one-hour tracks such as Birrawanna or Bobbin Head to tough whole day adventures, such as Jerusalem Bay to Brooklyn (part of the Great North Walk). To find out more about walking trac visit the Information Centre at Bobbin Head, open 1000-1600, T 9472 8949, or refer to our companion book *Sydney's Best Bush, Park & City Walks*.

you want to stay a little longer, there's bush camping at The Basin, ith sheltered gas barbecues, toilets, water and cold showers (for ervous swimmers, there's even a shark net across the bay). Unless ou walk in from West Head Road, The Basin isn't accessible by car. e best way to get there is by ferry or water taxi from Palm Beach.

There's also an abundance of scenic picnic areas. Some of the larger picnic areas are already written up in this book. However, you'll find other quiet spots at Akuna Bay, Apple Tree Bay, Brooklyn Dam, Duckhole Picnic Area and Salvation Creek Picnic Area. Although some of these spots have metal fireplaces, you're best to bring your own portable gas stove as open fires are banned at many times of year.

Sheoaks above Resolute Beach

73 McCarrs Creek Reserve

This spacious reserve lies alongside McCarrs Creek, with Ku-ring-gai Chase National Park on the opposite shore. Ample shade is provided by the figs and gums throughout the park and also by the mangroves on the water's edge. It is a lovely place for swimming (although the embankment can be steep in parts) with still shallow water, perfect for a lazy day on the lilo or for the kids to splash in. The flat open lawns make for a great play area.

At a glance

Address: McCarrs Creek Road, near Church Point

Map refs: G 168/A11, S 198/Q3, U 117/L11

Public transport: Buses E86, 155 and 156 all stop at McCarrs Creek

Parking: Metered between 0600-2100

Entry fee: None

Opening times: 24 hours

BBQs: Wood (wood provided)

Boating: No

Dogs: Leashed

Kiosk/café: No

Playground: No

Power/lights: No

Shade: Many trees

Swimming: Creek

Tables: Yes

Toilets: Yes

Water: Taps

Wheelchairs: Good access

74 West Head (Resolute Picnic Area)

The actual picnic spot here may not be the most scenic part of the 'Chase' but this is a great spot to use as a base for exploring the immediate area. Soak up the bush ambience, try local walks and explore the early aboriginal sites, and of course take in the spectacular views from the headland itself. Don't miss the 'Red Hand' caves just behind the picnic spot — some basic information is available on display boards. For the wildlife enthusiast there is plenty of opportunity to see native species, especially lizards, birds and maybe wallabies.

Lion Island from West Head

At a glance

Address: West Head Road, Ku-ring-gai Chase National Park

Map refs: G 109/A8, S 159/J8, U 78/F8

Public transport: None

Parking: Unrestricted during opening times

Entry fee: $11 for national park entry (or NPWS pass)

Opening times: Entry road open 0600-2030

BBQs: Gas (free)

Boating: No

Dogs: No

Kiosk/café: No

Playground: No

Power/lights: No

Shade: A few trees, sheltered table

Swimming: No

Tables: Yes

Toilets: Yes

Water: Taps

Wheelchairs: Toilet, good access

75 Resolute Beach

A definite hike (about half an hour each way from West Head, with many steps making it a walk for the sure-footed) is well compensated by this secluded, pristine and frequently deserted beach. Numerous aboriginal archeological engravings and cultural features can be found on the alternative access walk down from Resolute Picnic Spot (about an hour each way), making for a very pleasant circuit walk.

At a glance

Address: West Head Road, Ku-ring-gai Chase National Park

Map refs: G 109/D11, S 159/M11, U 78/J11

Public transport: Palm Beach Ferry (T 9974 1700) operates from 0900-1700 and drops off at nearby Great Mackerel Beach (800 m)

Parking: Unrestricted at West Head during opening times

Entry fee: $11 for vehicle entry (or NPWS pass)

Opening times: Entry road open 0600-2030

BBQs: No

Boating: No

Dogs: No

Kiosk/café: No

Playground: No

Power/lights: No

Shade: A few trees and high enclosing cliffs

Showers: No

Snorkelling: Yes

Surfing: No

Swimming: Harbour

Tables: No

Toilets: No

Water: No

Wheelchairs: No

76 The Basin

This natural basin is tucked into the west side of Pittwater and looks across to Barrenjoey Head. Access is either a pleasant but steep walk down from West Head Road (2.5 km each way) or via ferry from Palm Beach. Surrounded by Ku-ring-gai national Park, this open, grassy area comes complete with relaxed wallabies and lots of other wildlife. There is a function centre that can be booked for the larger events and a campsite with good, if basic, facilities. The Basin itself makes for great swimming but note that you can only anchor boats outside the Basin itself, which is open to Pittwater but netted off from the main harbour.

At a glance

Address: Ku-ring-gai Chase National Park

Map refs: G 138/J3, S 159/G19, U 98/A4

Public transport: Palm Beach Ferry (T 9974 1700) operates from 0900-1700 and drops off at the Basin Wharf ($12.40 adults/$6.40 concession & kids/free for under fives); The L90 and 190 buses stop near the wharf

Parking: Metered parking by Palm Beach Wharf

Entry fee: $3 adults, $2 for 5-15 yr olds ($4.40/$2.20 if walking) – camping $10 adults, $5 children includes entry

Opening times: 24 hours (but restricted ferry times)

Bookings: See www.nationalparks.nsw.gov.au for booking forms

BBQs: Gas (free) and wood (wood provided)

Boating: No

Dogs: No

Kiosk/café: No

Playground: No

Power/lights: No

Shade: Plenty of trees, some sheltered tables

Swimming: Yes

Tables: Yes

Toilets: Yes

Water: Bubblers/taps

Wheelchairs: Toilet, ferry access

Although actually quite large, this park nestles at the bottom of a small wooded valley and has a very snug feeling. Being in the middle of the Ku-ring-gai National Park, there's lots of wildlife to be seen, especially birds and lizards. Fishing and swimming can be found in Illawong Bay just over the road. This very serene park makes a nice spot to break from exploring the National Park.

At a glance

Address: Liberator General San Martin Drive, Ku-ring-gai Chase National Park

Map refs: G 166/B2, S 177/M14, U 116/G2

Public transport: None

Parking: Unrestricted during opening times

Entry fee: $11 for national park entry (or NPWS pass)

Opening times: 0600-2030

BBQs: Gas (free)

Boating: Ramp at nearby Akuna Bay

Dogs: No

Kiosk/café: At Akuna Bay

Playground: No

Power/lights: No

Shade: A few trees, sheltered tables

Swimming: Netted area in creek

Tables: Yes

Toilets: Yes

Water: Taps

Wheelchairs: Good access (toilet at Akuna Bay)

The shy echidna

Eastern water dragon

78 Ku-ring-gai Wildflower Garden

To leave the highway and step into Ku-ring-gai Wildflower Garden is to discover a special place, a world of tall forest, sandstone outcrops, ponds, gullies and waterfalls. There are three dedicated picnic areas within the park, linked by display gardens, ponds, boardwalks and walking tracks (some suitable for wheelchairs/strollers). There is also a visitor centre, which runs environmental education programs such as Bush Birthday Parties, School Programs, Bush Kids and Nature for the Very Young activities. Their Festival of Wildflowers is held every spring (usually the last weekend in August).

At a glance

Address: Mona Vale Road, St Ives

Map refs: G 224/F2, S 216/L6, U 155/F2

Public transport: 196 Forest Coach bus from Gordon Station (400 m)

Parking: Unrestricted car park during opening hours

Entry fee: Free

Opening times: 0800-1600 (or 1000-2400 for function bookings)

BBQs: Electric (free) at Dampiers and Lambers Clearings, and at Visitor Centre

Bookings: Ku-ring-gai Council, T 9440 8552 (up to 120 people)

Dogs: No

Kiosk: No

Playground: Yes, at Lamberts Clearing. Swings, slide, climbing frame, open field

Power/lights: No

Shade: Shelters at Lamberts Clearing and Visitor Centre

Swimming: No

Tables: Yes. Seating for up to 75 people

Toilets: Yes

Water: Taps

Wheelchairs: Toilets. Ramped paths to Dampiers Clearing and Visitor Centre. Accessible walking track.

At a glance

Address: Bobbin Head Road,
Ku-ring-gai Chase National Park

Map refs: G 163/J14, S 196/E6,
U 114/P14

Public transport: None

Parking: Unrestricted during
opening times

Entry fee: $11 per vehicle (or
NPWS pass)

Opening times: 0600-2030

BBQs: Gas (free)

Boating: No

Dogs: No

Kiosk/café: Bobbin Head Inn,
T 9472 8949

Playground: Swings, climbing
frames

Power/lights: No

Shade: Shelter areas, sheltered
tables

Swimming: Not recommended

Tables: Yes

Toilets: Yes

Water: Bubblers/taps

Wheelchairs: Toilet, good access

This picnic spot is nestled between hills of natural bushland and looks out over idyllic Apple Tree Bay. Central to the picnic ground is The Bobbin Inn, which has a friendly restaurant, café and gift/information shop with a good range of local guide books and Australiana. The rest of the park is big enough to cope with the busiest summer weekend and includes a large children's playground. There are a number of short walks from the park, shown on the information board across the road from the inn.

Galston Reserve playground

North West

The diversity of parks and reserves in Sydney's north-west is partly a reflection of the diversity of the landscape itself. The waters of Berowra Creek and the Nepean/Hawkesbury River wind through the rocky sandstone gorges of Galston and Berowra, contrasting against the rolling hills of the Cumberland Plains, and all flanked by the rugged water-dissected plateaus of Blue Mountains National Park.

The Cumberland Plains were very attractive to early European settlers. As Governor Phillip wrote in April 1788: 'The country through which we travelled was singularly fine, level, or rising in small hills of a very pleasing and picturesque appearance. The soil was excellent.' It is because of this fertile soil that Sydney's north-west is rich in colonial history, with historic homesteads at Cattai, Rouse Hill and Parramatta Park.

There are also several small national parks and significant nature reserves in the north west, including Bidjigal Reserve, Cattai National Park, Crosslands Reserve, Cumberland State Forest and Lake Parramatta. These parks may not be international drawcards in the way that the Blue Mountains or Royal National Park are, but they are the 'jewels' of the wild west, rightfully well-loved by locals and a delightful surprise to visitors.

Hawkesbury River

80 Berowra Waters

If you love water and mucking around on boats, this is the spot for you. From the marina on the north side of the water (which you cross on a small vehicular ferry) you can hire single kayaks, double kayaks, old-fashioned tinnies, or even a BBQ pontoon complete with toilet, icebox and awning. The Macquarie Princess is also available for charter (suitable for groups of 20-100). The picnic area next to the marina has good facilities, but many people prefer to take their boats and picnic at one of the many secret bays along Berowra Creek.

At a glance

Address: Berowra Waters Road, Berowra Waters

Map refs: G 132/F4, S 155/F19, U 94/A4

Public transport: None

Parking: Unrestricted car park

Entry fee: None

Opening times: 24 hours

BBQs: Electric (free)

Boating: Ramp; boat hire: T 9456 7000, www.berowrawaters.net; charter: Macquarie Princess Charters, T 4566 4455

Dogs: Leashed

Kiosk/café: Fish Café open 0900-2000 Wed-Sun, 0900-1500 Mon-Tue. Seafood buffet Fri-Sun, T 9456 4665.

Playground: Pirate ship and springy bounce animals

Power/lights: No

Shade: Several sheltered tables

Swimming: Yes, although not recommended immediately after heavy rain

Tables: Yes

Toilets: Yes

Water: Taps

Wheelchairs: Toilets and ramped paths

In 1856, Burton Crossland was one of the first settlers in the Hornsby area, and he built the first tracks from Crosslands Reserve to Hornsby and to Galston. Enclosed by steep Hawkesbury sandstone escarpments, this green stretch of river flats is still delightfully unspoilt, and ideal for birdwatching, camping, canoeing, fishing or for a family day out. Simple bush camping facilities are also available — however remember to bring insect repellent!

At a glance

Address: End of Somerville Road, Hornsby Heights

Map refs: G 132/A16, S 175/C11, J 93/L16

Public transport: None

Parking: Unrestricted car park, closes 1930

Entry fee: None

Opening times: 0730-1930

BBQs: Wood (sometimes, but not always supplied)

Boating: No boat ramp, but access for kayaks and non-motorised craft

Camping: $9 adult, $6 children, per night, plus $25 key deposit (if required), T 9847 6791

Dogs: No

Kiosk/café: No

Playground: Monkey bars, climbing frame, kid's bike track

Power/lights: No

Shade: Plenty of trees and several sheltered tables at each end of the reserve

Swimming: Not recommended, especially after heavy rain

Tables: Yes

Toilets: Yes

Water: No

Wheelchairs: Poor access to toilets; access across grass to picnic shelters

82 Fagan Park

Creeks, rolling hills, open paddocks and permaculture display gardens create a rural feel to this large and significant park. Walking tracks and cycleways connect picnic areas, children's playgrounds, formal gardens, pockets of remnant bushland and the inspiring 'Gardens of Many Nations'. Each garden has a theme from a different country, displaying plants and landscape styles from North America, South America, The Netherlands, England, Australia, Japan, China, Africa and the Mediterranean.

At a glance

Address: Arcadia Road, Galston

Map refs: G 159/F6, S 173/L17, U 112/A6

Public transport: Hillsbus 638 stops on Arcadia Rd near the entrance (300 m)

Parking: Car parks at southern and northern ends, close 1730

Entry fee: $4 per vehicle, $35 per coach

Opening times: 0700-1730 (1830 daylight saving)

BBQs: Lots of electric (free)

Boating: No

Bookings: From $85 for large picnic shelters, T 9847 6791

Dogs: Leashed

Kiosk/café: No (one is proposed for peak times however)

Playground: Two playgrounds, including swings, climbing frames, slides

Power/lights: No

Shade: Plenty of trees, many sheltered tables

Swimming: No

Tables: Yes, including shelter sheds for large groups

Toilets: Yes

Water: Bubblers

Wheelchairs: Toilets; grassy access to picnic tables; good network of paths

ydney history - Fagan Park

ne story of how Fagan Park came to exist is heart-warming. In 1979, Bruce
agan donated an area of about 55 hectares to the Department of Lands, with
ornsby Shire Council appointed as sole trustee for the park. In his Deed of Gift,
stated 'The Donor is desirous of the donation lands being preserved indefinitely
ter his lifetime and the lifetime of his sister for the cultural, recreational,
Jucational and historical benefit and use of the public.'

ne trustees have been faithful to this vision and adopted the park as the
Juncil's bicentennial project. Fagan Park was officially opened in November
88 and now visitors come from all over northern Sydney to spend the day
cnicking, walking, cycling, admiring the gardens or visiting the museum.

ne original Netherby homestead, farm buildings, packing shed, brick kiln site
id clay pit still stand. The homestead has been meticulously maintained in its
iginal state and there is now a Rural Museum which displays many types of
achinery used in past eras. The Netherby Homestead and Museum is open
'ery Tuesday and second Sunday of each month, T 9847 6853 for further
:tails.

83 Galston Recreation Reserve

This reserve is a great spot for large groups to get together for picnics, end-of-year parties and sports presentation days, featuring a large shelter shed with 18 tables and four electric BBQs that accommodates up to 150 people. The playground attracts children every day of the year with a whimsical tower structure and lots of tunnels, lookouts and slides. Adjacent sporting fields and basketball courts mean that this reserve gets very busy most weekends.

At a glance

Address: Galston Road, Galston

Map refs: G 159/D14, S 193/H6, U 111/Q14

Public transport: Hillsbus 638

Parking: Unrestricted car park

Entry fee: None

Opening times: 24 hours

BBQs: Electric (free) in shelter shed and gazebo, wood BBQs behind playground

Boating: No

Bookings: Shelter shed hire, $100 per day, T 9847 6791

Dogs: Leashed

Kiosk/café: No

Playground: Imaginative tower structure includes slides, climbing frames, lookouts and tunnels

Power/lights: No

Shade: Two sheltered tables (including shed), some trees

Sporting fields: Two basketball courts, oval, softball/baseball pitch

Swimming: At Galston District Aquatic Centre, next door

Tables: In shelter shed and gazebo, also uncovered tables behind playground

Toilets: Yes

Water: Taps

Wheelchairs: Toilet; ramped access to shelter shed

84 Wisemans Ferry Park

Next to the ferry crossing and perched on a bend in the Hawkesbury opposite the Macdonald River entrance, this park has plenty of BBQs, tables, shady picnic areas, fishing spots, open space for playing games and a sandy beach with shallow waters perfect for children to play in. Established in 1827, Wisemans Ferry crossing is the oldest ferry service in Australia. The village of Wisemans Ferry is rich in historical interest, as well as being a great destination for a family day out.

At a glance

Address: Old Northern Road, Wisemans Ferry

Map refs: S 92/G2, U 52/L9

Public transport: None

Parking: Unrestricted car park

Entry fee: None

Opening times: 24 hours

BBQs: Electric (free), wood (no wood provided)

Boating: Public wharf to the right of the ferry, just beyond park entrance. Houseboat hire also available, T 1800 024 979, www.hawkesburyhouseboats.com.au

Dogs: Leashed

Kiosk/café: Yes, home to the famous Bernie Burgers

Playground: Many see-saws, slides, swings, spring-bounce animals

Power/lights: No

Shade: Lots of trees, some sheltered tables

Swimming: Yes, safe paddling for children

Tables: Yes

Toilets: Yes

Water: Tap in toilet (rainwater tank water)

Wheelchairs: Toilet; good access

The Cattai Farm area was originally a land grant to First Fleet assistant surgeon Thomas Arndell. To this day, you can see the historic grain silos, windmill remains, convict-built road or visit Arndell's 1821 cottage (currently open Sundays only). Cattai has been a popular picnic destination since the 1930s, with lots of large shelters and barbecue areas along the banks of the Hawkesbury River, as well as a spacious shady campsite and wide open areas for children to run around and play.

At a glance

Address: Wisemans Ferry Road, Cattai

Map refs: G 64/B13, S 130/D17, U 50/L15

Public transport: None

Parking: Unrestricted car park, closes 1730

Entry fee: $7 per vehicle or NPWS pass

Opening times: 0730-1730 (1830 daylight saving)

BBQs: Wood (wood provided)

Boating: No (only tour boats can land, no launching or landing of other boats permitted)

Bookings: There are nine separate shelter shed areas, all suitable for large groups. T 4572 3100, $30 per booking.

Camping: Yes. Advance bookings essential, up to 2 weeks ahead. T 4572 3100. $5.00 per adult, $3.00 per child per night, plus standard entry fee

Dogs: No

Kiosk/café: No, but a mobile kiosk for weekends is planned

Playground: Two playgrounds, one near info centre, one by the river

Power/lights: No

Shade: Plenty of trees, lots of sheltered tables

Swimming: Water quality is variable, T 4560 4444 for more info

Tables: Yes

Toilets: Yes

Water: Taps

Wheelchairs: Toilet and showers (by camping area); reasonable access to many areas (ask when booking)

Separated from the main Cattai picnic areas by several kilometres of road, Mitchell Park tends to be a quiet spot, attracting couples and small families rather than large groups. Although facilities are simple, Mitchell Park attracts many birdwatchers and nature enthusiasts. The surrounding park features a variety of plant communities (including rare riverine rainforest), an extensive network of walking tracks, and a field studies centre which is used by university, school and community groups.

At a glance

Address: Mitchell Park Road, Cattai

Map refs: G 94/K4, S 150/N3, U 69/B4

Public transport: None

Parking: Unrestricted car park, closes 1730

Entry fee: $7 per vehicle or NPWS pass

Opening times: 0730-1730 (1830 daylight saving)

BBQs: Wood (no wood provided)

Boating: No

Dogs: No

Kiosk/café: No

Playground: No

Power/lights: No

Shade: Plenty of trees, sheltered tables

Swimming: Not recommended due to sewerage treatment plant upstream

Tables: Yes

Toilets: Yes

Water: Bubblers outside toilets

Wheelchairs: Toilets next to picnic area 2; access to picnic areas across grassy paddock; first 300 metres of walking trail is wheelchair-friendly

Once part of the sprawling Rouse Hill Estate (another part of which is operated by the Heritage Houses Trust, see opposite), this large area has been gradually converted to parkland. It now comprises some woodland, accessible via various bushtracks, a couple of huge grassy areas, several picnic areas and some of the most imaginative playgrounds in Sydney, complete with a rare flying fox. There are two large pavilions that can be booked by groups. The facilities are generally very good, though the toilets are composting and not always easy on the nose!

At a glance

Address: Worcester Road, Rouse Hill

Map refs: G 184/G8, S 190/H15, U 128/M8

Public transport: Buses 746 (stops on Windsor, 1.3 km) or 741 (stops on Rouse Road, 800 m)

Parking: Unrestricted car park, closes 1700 (1900 daylight saving)

Entry fee: None

Opening times: 0800-2000

BBQs: Electric (free)

Boating: No

Bookings: Two pavilions can be booked. See www.nationalparks.nsw.gov.au for application forms

Dogs: Leashed

Kiosk/café: No

Playground: Swings, climbing frame, ropes, slides, flying fox

Power/lights: Power in pavilions

Shade: Some trees, some sheltered tables

Swimming: No

Tables: Yes

Toilets: Yes

Water: Taps (needs boiling to drink)

Wheelchairs: Toilet; good access

Out and about
in Rouse Hill

Rouse Hill Estate

Completed in 1818, Rouse Hill was built as a gentleman farmer's residence by convict labour for the original settlers Richard and Elizabeth Rouse. It was occupied by the Rouse family for over 180 years, and is one of the oldest buildings in New South Wales. The house can be visited on a guided tour, which also encompasses the outbuildings and gardens, creating a vivid picture of the history of Australian country life over nearly two centuries. The building is fragile, hence tours are limited: Wed, Thu and Sun only, various times between 1000 and 1400. Tour groups are limited to 15 people. Entry $8, children $4 (www.hht.net.au, T 9627 6777).

Two great pubs

Rouse Hill and neighbouring Kellyville are home to two of Sydney's most iconic pubs. The Mean Fiddler dates back nearly as far as Rouse Hill, first opening its doors (as the Royal Oak) in 1826, and entering its current incarnation just over 10 years ago. Living up to its name, it's famous for live music and now sprawls over several bars and beer gardens, from the carefully restored original pub bars to the huge new replica Woolshed (though we doubt any traditional woolshed ever got quite this lively!). Just up the road is one of the most photographed pubs in Australia, The Ettamogah. There are actually four of these (the first one was built in Albury) and they were inspired by the long running cartoon series pencilled by Ken Maynard.

88 Governor Phillip Park

This park may not be a drawcard for nature lovers seeking peace and solitude, but it's enormously popular with locals because of the wide boat ramp and excellent access for motor boats, jet skis, water skis, wake-boards, and anything else that moves fast and makes a lot of noise. Picnickers can enjoy the hubbub of the boating scene, as well as the electric BBQs, covered shelters and excellent children's playground.

At a glance

Address: George Street (beyond Terrace Motel), Windsor

Map refs: G 121/G5, S 168/L1, U 86/M5

Public transport: Buses 675 or 767 from Windsor Station to town centre (800 m)

Parking: Unrestricted car park

Entry fee: None

Opening times: 24 hours

BBQs: Electric (free)

Boating: Yes

Dogs: Leashed

Kiosk/café: The Upper Hawkesbury Power Boat Club clubhouse (open some weekends and during special events)

Playground: Swings, mini-climbing wall, tunnel, spider web climb, slides

Power/lights: No

Shade: Some trees, two large shelters (both with tables and BBQs)

Swimming: Not recommended

Tables: Yes

Toilets: Yes

Water: Bubbler/taps

Wheelchairs: Toilet; good access

89 Navua Reserve

At a glance

Address: End of Grose River Road, Grose Wold

Map refs: G 116/G10, S 165/J6, U83/G10

Public transport: None

Parking: Unrestricted car park, closes 2000

Entry fee: None

Opening times: 0730-2000

BBQs: Wood (wood not provided)

Boating: No boat ramp, but access for non-motorised craft

Dogs: Leashed

Kiosk/café: No

Playground: No

Power/lights: No

Shade: Plenty of trees

Swimming: Yes

Tables: Yes

Toilets: Yes

Water: Bubbler

Wheelchairs: Toilets; grassy access to picnic areas; no access to water

Navua Reserve is on the banks of the Grose River, just before the Grose meets up with the Nepean/Hawkesbury. As the Grose runs straight down from the Blue Mountains National Park, the water here is much cleaner than any other rivers in the Richmond area, and so is ideal for swimming. Children love to paddle on the sandy banks, dogs frolic in the shallows and fishermen find quiet spots further upstream. Long avenues of trees with flat grassy areas underneath are ideal for games, picnics and languorous afternoon snoozes.

90 Yellow Rock Lookout

Pick a warm summer's evening, pack a gourmet picnic hamper, throw in a fine bottle of wine and invite that special person in your life to a mystery destination. With views stretching for miles over the Cumberland Plains from a picnic table perched on a lonely rocky outcrop, romance will surely blossom as the sparkling stars emerge.

At a glance

Address: Yellow Rock Road, via Singles Ridge Road, Winmalee

Map refs: G 175/A10, S 184/J18, U 122/F10

Public transport: None

Parking: Unrestricted car park

Entry fee: None

Opening times: 24 hours

BBQs: No

Boating: No

Dogs: Leashed

Kiosk/café: No

Playground: No (parents, beware of unfenced cliffs)

Power/lights: No

Shade: One shelter, other areas surrounded by bush

Swimming: No

Tables: Yes

Toilets: No

Water: No

Wheelchairs: No

When the feeling of the city starts to work its way into your very bones, it's time to head to a place where the air smells of eucalyptus and where views stretch for miles. To a place where the sound of traffic has finally disappeared and instead, you can hear the sound of your own heart beating. The picnic facilities at Martins Lookout may be simple (non-existent, actually!) but the surroundings are quite simply food for the soul.

At a glance

Address: End of Farm Road, Springwood

Map refs: G 202/C13, S 202/N20, U(Blue Mountains section) 26/H16

Public transport: None

Parking: Unrestricted car park

Entry fee: None

Opening times: 24 hours

BBQs: No

Boating: No

Dogs: No

Kiosk/café: No

Playground: No

Power/lights: No

Shade: Not much at the lookout, lots down by the creek

Swimming: A 20 minute (steep) bushwalk leads to the turquoise-coloured waterholes of Glenbrook Creek

Tables: No

Toilets: No

Water: No

Wheelchairs: No

92 Tench Reserve

Tench Reserve stretches for 2.5 kilometres along the eastern bank of the Nepean River, with the Nepean Belle departure point positioned conveniently at the southern end. Ample shade, lots of grassy open spaces, two playgrounds, electric BBQs (you need to get in early on the weekend) and a boat ramp make this a great place for families. To complete your day out, combine a picnic with a paddlewheeler cruise (T 4733 1274, www.nepeanbelle.com.au), and discover the remarkable wilderness of the Nepean Gorge.

At a glance

Address: Tench Avenue, Jamisontown

Map refs: G 235/G14, S 224/P15, U 162/M14

Public transport: None close

Parking: Unrestricted car park

Entry fee: None

Opening times: 24 hours

BBQs: Electric (free)

Boating: Yes (ramp open 0500-2000 summer, 0900-1800 winter)

Dogs: Leashed

Kiosk/café: No

Playground: Two areas, both with swings, climbing frames, slides

Power/lights: Park lighting

Shade: Wide canopy trees, sheltered tables

Swimming: Not recommended (strong currents, fluctuating water quality)

Tables: Yes

Toilets: Yes, at southern end only

Water: Taps

Wheelchairs: Toilets; good access to picnic areas

93 Sydney International Regatta Centre

With 196 hectares of landscaped and native parkland, the Regatta Centre — also known as Penrith Lakes — is one of the best rowing and sprint kayak courses in the world. An average of 50,000 visitors come here every month to watch sporting events, go skydiving, or to walk, cycle or jog around the network of paths. A picnic here is best enjoyed when an event is on, T 4730 0000 or visit www.regattacentre.com.au for details.

At a glance

Address: Penrith Lakes, Castlereagh Rd, Penrith

Map refs: G 205/J13, S 204/R17, 142/P13

Public transport: None (shuttle buses run during major events)

Parking: Unrestricted car park, closes sunset

Entry fee: None (except during major events)

Opening times: Sunrise to sunset

BBQs: Gas (free) on Southern Bank

Boating: Canoe hire, T 4730 4000, Wed to Sun

Bookings: Yes, T 4730 0000 ($165/day)

Dogs: Leashed

Fishing: Catch and release program, Sun & Tues, 0900-1700

Kiosk/café: Regatta Kitchen & Bar, T 4729 3222. Open whenever events are on

Playground: No

Power/lights: Yes

Shade: Covered BBQ areas

Swimming: No

Tables: Yes

Toilets: Yes

Water: Bubbler/taps

Wheelchairs: Showers; toilets; ramps; specialist sailing facilities and tactile ground surface indicators

94 Nurragingy Reserve

This very large reserve is not only culturally significant to the local Aboriginal community, but also contains important bushland remnants of Grey Box and Forest Red Gum open forest, which is where most of the many picnic areas are found. Also part of the reserve are some lawns, formal gardens, pavilions and a large lake fronting the commercial Colebee Centre. This large reception building is where the toilets and kiosk are located. Several bushwalks thread through the reserve, though the maze of roads means none are very long. Nurragingy does get very busy on a sunny weekend.

At a glance

Address: Knox Road, Doonside

Map refs: G 242/K13, S 229/H12, U 167/K13

Public transport: Doonside Station (800 m)

Parking: Unrestricted car park, closes 1700 (1900 daylight saving)

Entry fee: None

Opening times: Closes 1700 (1900 daylight saving)

BBQs: Wood (wood provided)

Boating: No

Dogs: Leashed

Kiosk/café: At Colebee Centre; open at weekends generally 1000-1600, not when raining

Playground: Several; swings, climbing frame, ropes, slides

Power/lights: No

Shade: Plenty of trees, some sheltered tables

Swimming: No

Tables: Many

Toilets: Yes, at Colebee Centre

Water: Taps

Wheelchairs: Good access

95 Crestwood Reserve

At a glance

Address: Chapel Lane, Baulkham Hills

Map refs: G 246/K5, S 231/R5, U 170/E5

Public transport: None close

Parking: Unrestricted car park

Entry fee: None

Opening times: 24 hours

BBQs: Electric (free)

Boating: No

Dogs: Off leash

Kiosk/café: No

Playground: Climbing frames, ropes, slides

Power/lights: No

Shade: Plenty of trees, some sheltered tables

Swimming: No

Tables: Yes

Toilets: Yes

Water: Taps

Wheelchairs: Toilet; good access

This suburban park manages to go several notches above the usual standard with a well thought out combination of recreational sports areas, open woodland and large grassy areas. There's also a skate park and separate skateboard area, and plenty of picnic and BBQ facilities. There are cycle paths and walkways throughout, and they connect with a series of green corridors that extend several kilometres to the south and east.

A relatively small park, Castle Hill manages to give a real feel of space, thanks to a couple of large, rolling grassy areas, fringed mostly by woodland. The picnic and play areas are modern and well laid out, though the designers chose to leave out toilets and BBQs. The exact origins of the name have been lost, but what is sure is that the area was the site of the first European 'uprising' on Australian soil in 1804. The park commemorates the event, as well as the various different elements of the community that lived in the area when it was first established as a 'Government farm'.

At a glance

Address: Heritage Park Drive or Banks Road, Castle Hill

Map refs: G 218/F8, S 212/R13, U 151/F8

Public transport: Buses to Castle Hill Towers (1.4 km)

Parking: Unrestricted car park

Entry fee: None

Opening times: 24 hours

BBQs: None

Boating: No

Dogs: Leashed

Kiosk/café: No

Playground: Climbing frames and ropes; shaded

Power/lights: No

Shade: Some trees, some sheltered tables

Swimming: No

Tables: Yes

Toilets: No

Water: Taps

Wheelchairs: Good access

97 Cumberland State Forest

The only state forest in any Australian metropolitan area, Cumberland Forest is well-loved by families, birdwatchers and nature-lovers. Management of the land was taken over by the then NSW Forestry Commission in 1938 and a visionary arboretum was planted, featuring native trees from all around Australia. Visitor facilities are well thought-out and inviting, from the forest-shrouded picnic areas to the information centre and native plant nursery. There are several walking trails and rangers run a series of activities including spotlighting tours and bushtucker tastings. See www.dpi.nsw.gov.au/forests or T 9871 3377.

At a glance

Address: Castle Hill Road, West Pennant Hills

Map refs: G 249/E2, S 233/K3, U 171/Q2

Public transport: Hillsbus 634, 635 & 636

Parking: Unrestricted car park, closes 1700 (1800 daylight saving)

Entry fee: None

Opening times: 0830-1700 (1800 daylight saving)

BBQs: Electric (free)

Boating: No

Dogs: Leashed

Kiosk/café: Café Saligny, part of the information centre, open Tue-Sun 0930-1630

Playground: No

Power/lights: No

Shade: Plenty of trees, some sheltered tables

Swimming: No

Tables: Yes

Toilets: Yes, at information centre

Water: Bubblers

Wheelchairs: Toilet; good access; sesory forest trail

Bidjigal Reserve is the jewel in the crown of the reserves in this area of Sydney, with 300 hectares of bushland, over 370 native plant species and more than 140 native animals. Ted Horwood Reserve is one of two picnic areas (the other is off Ferguson Avenue), and is well-positioned between tennis courts, soccer fields, a playground and a community nursery. The highlight is the network of bushwalks that winds around the reserve, through sheltered rainforest gullies and tall eucalypt forest.

At a glance

Address: Park Road, Baulkham Hills

Map refs: G 248/C12, S 232/P12, U 171/C12

Public transport: None close

Parking: Unrestricted car park

Entry fee: None

Opening times: 24 hours

BBQs: Electric (free)

Boating: No

Dogs: Leashed

Kiosk/café: Tuckshop open on sport days

Playground: Climbing frame, slides, swings

Power/lights: No

Shade: Plenty of trees, some covered tables

Sporting grounds: Tennis courts, soccer pitch, basketball court, cricket pitch

Swimming: No

Tables: Yes

Toilets: Yes

Water: Taps

Wheelchairs: Not easy access

At a glance

Address: Entrance off Lackey Street, North Parramatta

Map refs: G 278/D8, S 252/P4, U 191/D8

Public transport: Hillsbus 609

Parking: Unrestricted car park, closes 1730

Entry fee: None

Opening times: 0630-1730 (1930 daylight saving)

BBQs: Electric (free)

Boating: Yes (non-powered craft)

Dogs: Leashed

Kiosk/café: Open Tue-Fri 0900-1430, Sat-Sun 0800-1700

Playground: Climbing frame, slide, liberty swing

Power/lights: No

Shade: Plenty of trees, several sheltered tables

Swimming: On Council-approved days only

Tables: Yes

Toilets: Yes

Water: Taps

Wheelchairs: Toilets; good access; Liberty swing

Older locals from almost anywhere in western Sydney will remember frolicking as children in the blue-green waters of Lake Parramatta, a popular swimming spot from 1909 right up till the 1970s. Although water was deemed unfit for swimming until recently, the quality is now good enough to allow swimming on council-approved dates. Even on days when swimming isn't officially authorised, the lake remains a great spot to depart on pirate adventures aboard home-made rafts.

Parramatta Park is one of the largest parks in western Sydney, attracting over one million people every year. The scene there is always full of life, with people riding bikes, rollerblading, walking, jogging, playing cricket or getting together for picnics and a relaxing time outdoors. The park is also a site of national cultural heritage significance, containing not only evidence of Aboriginal occupation but also Old Governor's House and the Dairy Cottage, two of the oldest remaining buildings in Australia.

At a glance

Address: Cnr Macquarie & Pitt Streets, Parramatta

Map refs: G 277/K16, S 252/K12, U 190/Q16

Public transport: Westmead Station (500 m), Parramatta Ferry (1.2 km)

Parking: Unrestricted parking, closes 1800

Entry fee: None

Opening times: 0600-1800 (2000 during daylight saving)

BBQs: Electric (free) at Coleman Oval, Salters Field, Pavilion Flat, The Picnic Ground and West Domain

Boating: No

Booking: There are 13 different picnic areas that can be booked, suitable for groups of 35 or more. Rates start from $110

Dogs: Leashed

Kiosk/café: Open daily, 0800-1600, T 9630 0144

Playground: Yes, at Pavilion Flat and Salters Field

Power/lights: In some areas

Shade: Lots of trees and sheltered tables

Swimming: Parramatta Swimming Centre, T 9630 3669, located on eastern edge of park

Tables: Yes

Toilets: Yes

Water: Bubbler/taps

Wheelchairs: Toilet; good access

Ghost tours at Government House

Sydney history – Old Government House

Parramatta Park is not only one of the earliest sites of Aboriginal/European contact, but also contains the oldest remaining public building in Australia: Old Government House. Every Governor from Phillip to Fitzroy spent some time enjoying this country retreat at Parramatta, preferring the clean air of rural lands to the 'chaotic filth' of city life.

The existing building was constructed in 1799 by Governor Hunter, and replaced the original small house that was built in 1790 for Governor Phillip. The building was extended in 1815 by Governor Macquarie and transformed the house into the elegant English style that visitors to the property can still observe today. Rooms are furnished with pieces from the National Trust's collection of early colonial furniture, and together comprise the largest collection of colonial furniture in Australia.

The building was restored by the Trust as a Vice-Regal residence in 1995 and is open for guided tours and functions, including the rather whimsical ghost tours that run on the 3rd Friday of each month during the evenings. Regular opening hours are Mon-Fr, 1000-1600, weekends & public holidays 1030-1600. Entry fees adults $8, concessions $5 (National Trust members free). T 9635 8149.

Pink paper daisies at Mount Annan Botanic Gardens

South West

The southwest of Sydney has a lot going for it. Not only does this area — along with the rest of western Sydney — have the fastest economic growth of anywhere in Australia, but it also has enormous cultural and ethnic diversity. As you explore the parks in this next few pages, you'll see Lebanese family groups with lavish picnic spreads, Pacific Islanders congregating to play no-holds-barred footie, Vietnamese extended families fishing from secluded bridges, local Buddhists scattering rose petals from river platforms, and much more besides.

Binding these scenes together, the sleepy Georges River snakes it way through the suburbs, with narrow waters and quiet swimming holes upstream, opening out to wider waters and inviting inlets downstream. Further west, the Nepean cuts through the base of the plateau at the foot of the Blue Mountains, with several of the wilder picnic spots perched on rocky outcrops looking down to the waters of the gorge below.

Oatley Park

101 Auburn Botanic Gardens

Part of a long string of playing fields, reserves and a golf course alongside the Duck River, the Botanic Gardens consists of several flora and fauna areas, including a fauna reserve, native gardens, rose gardens, rainforest and a series of Japanese gardens. The main picnic area is just outside and beyond the main entrance to the gardens, on the top of the steep bank down to the river. Large grassed areas are interspersed with several shelters and wooded areas. A riverside track can be followed north for about two kilometres.

At a glance

Address: Chiswick Road, Auburn

Map refs: G 338/H6, S 273/B14, U 231/H6

Public transport: Auburn Station (2.5 km), Transit First bus 909 (stops at station) to Cumberland Rd (700 m)

Parking: Unrestricted, but closed off from 1700 (1900 daylight saving)

Entry fee: None to picnic area; Gardens $2 for non-Auburn residents over 16

Opening times: Picnic area 24 hours; Gardens 0900-1700 (1900 weekends during daylight saving)

BBQs: Electric (free) in picnic area

Boating: No

Dogs: No

Kiosk/café: No

Playground: Swings, climbing frames, slides – both in picnic area and in the Gardens

Power/lights: No

Shade: Some trees, some sheltered tables in picnic area

Swimming: No

Tables: Many in picnic area

Toilets: Yes

Water: Taps

Wheelchairs: Toilets, good access

The Reflection Pool in the Gardens

102 Central Gardens

A great deal of thought went into planning Central Gardens, with the result that this is one of the best inland small parks in Sydney, despite being in the crook of two major roads. The best of the facilities are in the furthest corner of the park, where the traffic noise is minimal. A large grassy area is surrounded in turn by bush-fringed artificial ponds, an (occasional) kiosk, a series of modest wildlife enclosures (kangaroos, emus, cockatoos, wallabies), a very good playground, picnic and BBQ areas, amenities block and tennis courts (court hire, T 9637 9925).

At a glance

Address: Paton Street, Merrylands West

Map refs: G 306/H11, S 271/P3, J 210/C11

Public transport: From Merrylands Station, Hillsbus 811 to Merrylands Rd (200 m) or 812 to Coolibah St (300 m)

Parking: Unrestricted car park

Entry fee: None

Opening times: Closes 1900

BBQs: Electric (free)

Boating: No

Dogs: No

Kiosk/café: Open on an ad hoc basis, usually Sundays

Playground: Swings, climbing frame, ropes, slides; shaded

Power/lights: Some lighting

Shade: Plenty of trees, some sheltered tables

Swimming: No

Tables: Yes

Toilets: Yes

Water: Bubblers, taps by toilets, including boiling water

Wheelchairs: Toilet; good access

Since 1996, over 100,000 trees have been planted in the 600 hectares that make up Western Sydney Regional Park, slowly transforming this rolling farmland into very scenic parkland. Highlights include three platforms that look down over the inventive, interactive play area, each one well-equipped with electric BBQs and covered to provide welcome shade. Two kilometres of walking and cycling tracks fan out from the picnic area.

At a glance

Address: Cnr The Horsley Drive and Cowpasture Road, Bossley Park

Map refs: G 333/F4, S 269/M12, U 227/P4

Public transport: From Fairfield Station, Westbus bus 828 stops near the main gate

Parking: Unrestricted car park, closes at 1900

Entry fee: None

Opening times: 0800-1900

BBQs: Electric (free) on covered platforms

Boating: No

Dogs: Leashed

Kiosk/café: No

Playground: Interactive adventure playground for toddlers; rare flying fox and climbing equipment for older children

Power/lights: No

Shade: Some trees, BBQ shelters

Swimming: No

Tables: Yes

Toilets: Yes

Water: Bubblers

Wheelchairs: Toilet; good access

104 Euroka

Euroka is a great place to take overseas visitors for a picnic, as you're almost guaranteed to see eastern grey kangaroos sleeping under shady gums or grazing in the grassy clearings. Positioned at the foot of the Blue Mountains, and within the National Park, Euroka is the site of an ancient volcanic vent formed at least 150 million years ago. Cool creeks, lots of barbecues and picnic tables and a network of bushwalk trails provide something for all the family, and, if you're keen to stay longer, you can even camp overnight.

At a glance

Address: The Oaks Fire Trail, Glenbrook

Map refs: G 263/K15, S 243/N11, U 181/K15

Public transport: None close (Glenbrook Station 5.5 km away)

Parking: Unrestricted, closes 1800 (1900 daylight saving)

Entry fee: $7 per vehicle (or NPWS pass)

Opening times: 0830-1800 (1900 daylight saving) unless camping

BBQs: Wood (wood provided), but check in advance regarding fire restrictions. Portable gas BBQs with legs also permitted.

Camping: $5 adults, $3 children. Must be pre-booked, T 4588 5247

Dogs: No

Kiosk/café: No

Playground: No

Power/lights: No

Shade: Plenty of trees, some sheltered tables

Swimming: At the Nepean River, 1.2 km away via bushtrails

Tables: Yes

Toilets: Yes

Water: No (though there's a tap at the park entrance)

Wheelchairs: Not good access

Blue Mountains National Park

Some picnic areas in the southwestern section of this book are to be found in the Blue Mountains National Park, one of the most cherished of all Australia's wilderness areas. One million hectares right on the edge of our biggest city, this World Heritage area is a landscape of deep gorges, rugged valleys, wild creeks and significant biodiversity.

Although it's fun to drive up to the Blue Mountains, visit a café and go to a few lookouts, the best way to see the area is to ditch your car and get out in the bush. The visitor centres at both Glenbrook and Blackheath have lots of information about walking tracks (T 1300 653 408 or 4787 8877) or alternatively, *Blue Mountains Best Bushwalks*, a companion title to this book, describes over 60 bushwalks in the Blue Mountains.

Erskine Creek

Blue Mountains National Park

If you plan to stay in the Blue Mountains overnight, then you're probably best to head to the Upper Mountains (between Wentworth Falls and Mount Victoria) where the canyons are deeper, views more expansive and the heritage of the towns a little more interesting. However, for short day trips or picnics, the Lower Mountains are perfect. The warmer climate of Glenbrook lends itself to wonderfully lazy summer bushwalks, where you can wander a kilometre or two down to a swimming hole, relax for a few hours and then wend your way back home.

Grinding grooves near Campfire Creek

Entry to most areas of the Blue Mountains National Park is free, though if you enter by the Glenbrook gates, there's a charge of $7 per vehicle. Glenbrook is a good spot for day trips however, as not only can you visit Euroka to see the kangaroos and have a picnic, but you can plunge into Jellybean Pool or Blue Pool on your way out.

Tracks are susceptible to closures, and the gates at Glenbrook are sometimes locked on occasions, even during regular opening hours, as the causeway is prone to flooding. Phone 4787 8877 for more details about track or park closures. If you're planning a barbecue in summer, you'll also want to check current fire restrictions (T 4782 2159 or www.bluemountains.rfs.nsw.gov.au) as in conditions of total bans no BBQs of any kind are permitted (even using portable gas stoves).

If you want to stay a little longer — and stay out in the bush — there's car camping at Euroka (see the Euroka picnic entry on the previous page) and at Murphys Glen near Woodford. Alternatively check out www.bluemountainsaustralia.com for other accommodation options.

105 The Rock Lookout

Just north of Wallacia, a sign points to Nepean Gorge Lookout. Six kilometres of bitumen, two of dirt, a short walk of about 400 metres from the car park and a flight of precipitous stone steps leads to a bare rocky outcrop with magnificent views stretching north and south down to the gorge some distance below. So long as you don't get vertigo, and you leave any toddlers at home, this is an idyllic spot to spread out a blanket and while away a couple of hours.

At a glance

Address: Fairlight Road, Mulgoa

Map ref: S 243/Q19, U 201/L6, Fairlight Rd begins G 295/B16

Public transport: None

Parking: Unrestricted car park

Entry fee: None

Opening times: 24 hours

BBQs: No

Boating: No

Dogs: No (although everyone does)

Kiosk/café: No

Playground: No

Power/lights: No

Shade: Shaded track, exposed lookout

Swimming: No

Tables: One table by car park

Toilets: No

Water: No

Wheelchairs: No access

106 Blaxlands Crossing Reserve

Despite being so close to Penrith, this reserve feels very rural, with views stretching along the wide waters of the Nepean, mature eucalypts with wide canopies and horse jumps in adjacent paddocks. On warm summer evenings, this is a lovely spot to spend a couple of hours while the kids run around or alternatively, an adjacent caravan park makes this a possible overnight stop for weary travellers.

Mature eucalypts provide welcome shade

At a glance

Address: Silverdale Road, Wallacia

Map refs: G 324/H12, S 264/F20, U 222/C12

Public transport: From Penrith Station, Westbus bus 795 (200 m)

Parking: Unrestricted car park, closes 1700

Entry fee: $6 on weekends and public holidays

Opening times: 0800-1700

BBQs: Lots of wood BBQs, one large electric BBQ area suitable for large groups

Boating: No boat ramp, but non-motored craft can access the river at the adjacent Fowler Reserve

Camping: Wallacia Caravan Park, T4773 8077

Dogs: No

Kiosk/café: No

Playground: Swings, climbing frame, slides

Power/lights: No

Shade: Plenty of trees, many sheltered tables

Swimming: Access from adjacent Fowler Reserve, adults only (strong currents)

Tables: Yes

Toilets: Yes

Water: Taps

Wheelchairs: Not good access

Bents Basin is a deep waterhole in a gorge on the Nepean River between Camden and Penrith. Over 250 metres long, 140 metres wide, 22 metres deep, and almost completely encircled by high rugged cliffs, this popular spot draws people from all over Western Sydney. On weekends you'll see big family groups picnicking and swimming, mucking around on lilos and snoozing under casuarina trees. For interesting info about the history of Bents Basin, visit the area office that's on the left as you enter (0900-1700, weekdays only).

At a glance

Address: Bents Basin Road, Wallacia or Wolstenholme Avenue, Greendale

Map refs: G 384/G10, S 304/E9, U 262/B10

Public transport: None

Parking: Unrestricted car park, closes 1800

Entry fee: $7 per vehicle

Opening times: 0900-1800

BBQs: Electric (free) at the car park, wood (wood provided) next to the waterhole

Boating: Yes

Bookings: $27.50 to reserve spaces for large groups, T 4774 8662

Camping: Bents Basin campground T 4774 8662

Dogs: No

Kiosk/café: Open peak periods onl

Playground: No

Power/lights: No

Shade: Plenty of trees around the waterhole

Swimming: In waterhole

Tables: Yes

Toilets: Yes

Water: Taps

Wheelchairs: Toilets but no access to waterhole

108 Harrington Park

Harrington Park is one of the new 'designer' suburbs of the west, where green space, housing, schools, shopping, sporting facilities and transport are integrated as part of a single plan. This picnic area is on the edge of a small lake around which runs a shared cycleway and walkway. Younger children love this spot — especially the pirate ship — and locals like to stretch their legs walking around the lake. The suburb is named after adventurer Captain Campbell, who, when convicts stole his ship *The Harrington* in 1808, was compensated by a land grant in the area.

At a glance

Address: Royal George Drive, Harrington Park

Map ref: G 478/D3, S 346/K11, U324/J3

Public transport: From Campbelltown Station, Busways bus 894 stops on the corner of Harrington Pkwy and Sir Warwick Fairfax Dr (700 m)

Parking: Unrestricted

Entry fee: None

Opening times: 24 hours

BBQs: Electric (free)

Boating: No

Dogs: Leashed

Kiosk/café: No

Playground: Swings and pirate ship; basketball courts, football pitch

Power/lights: Only on basketball courts

Shade: Plenty of trees, one large shelter

Swimming: No (for black swans and ducks only!)

Tables: Yes

Toilets: Yes, but may be locked when clubhouse closed

Water: No

Wheelchairs: Toilet (if open); good access on paths around lake

109 Mount Annan Botanic Gardens

In the surrounding hot and noisy plains, Mount Annan Botanic Garden appears as an oasis, with display gardens of over 4,000 native species set in 410 hectares of hills and lakes. As well as a delightful restaurant and informative visitor centre, there are four picnic areas, each one with good shelters and free BBQs. Alternatively, the grassy banks of Lake Sedgewick and the rainforest-like surrounds of Banksia Garden make for peaceful spots to while away a warm afternoon.

At a glance

Address: Mount Annan Drive, Mount Annan

Map refs: Entrance G 509/H4, S 367/H8, U 345/H4

Public transport: From Campbelltown station, Busways 896 stops on the corner of Narellan Rd and Mt Annan Dr (2 km). Shuttle buses from station on Sundays, T 4634 7935

Parking: Unrestricted car park, closes 1600 (1800 summer)

Entry fee: Adults $4.40, seniors $3.30, child concession $2.20, family of four, $8.80

Opening times: 1000-1600 Apr-Sep; 1000-1800 Oct-Mar

Bookings: For large groups, including weddings, T 4634 2477

BBQs: Electric (free) at all four picnic areas

Boating: No

Dogs: No

Kiosk/café: Open for breakfast on weekends, lunch 7 days, and dinner Friday and Sunday

Playground: Flying fox, roundabout, sandpit, climbing frames. School holiday activities T 4648 2477

Power/lights: No

Shade: Covered shelters, each seating up to 40. Ample shade throughout the gardens, some available for hire

Swimming: No

Tables: Yes, at all four picnic areas

Toilets: Yes

Water: Taps

Wheelchairs: Toilets, good access Wheelchair hire available from Visitor Centre.

Sydney environment - The Wollemi Pine

In September 1994 David Noble, a local bushwalker, was exploring a canyon in the remote Wollemi National Park when he found some trees he didn't recognise. It soon became apparent that this was a great botanical discovery. Now known as Wollemia nobilis or the Wollemi Pine, this 'living fossil' is a strange looking tree. It grows to about 40 metres high, with upright branches developing from both the base and along the trunk, and has particularly unusual bumpy chocolate-bubble bark. This species is so old it's mind-boggling, with the oldest known Wollemi Pine type fossil dating back 90 million years, and some believe that the pines may date back to the Jurassic period.

Despite intensive searches, the Wollemi hasn't been found anywhere else other than in this narrow canyon and if anything should happen to this stand of fewer than 100 trees the species would become extinct in the wild. For this reason, the original location is kept a closely guarded secret.

A large specimen sits immediately outside the Gardens Visitor Centre, plus there's the Wollemi Walk of Discovery at the southern end of the gardens. This consists of about 80 trees at the moment but will continue to grow with further plantings. The trees grow very slowly, but in a few decades time, this grove of trees will tower high against the surrounding landscape, offering the public the unique experience of being able to walk amongst these incredible trees in the wild.

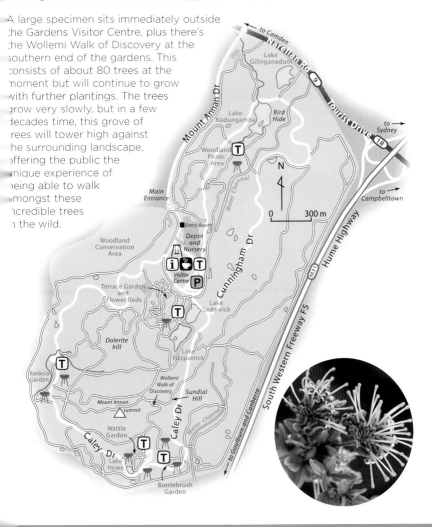

To walk into the Campbelltown Art Gallery Japanese Gardens is like stepping into a picture postcard. Pathways wind down to a small waterfall and simple pond, framed by a garden of immaculately trimmed hedges and meticulously chosen feature trees. Twin gazebos constructed in Japanese style provide shelter and a footbridge connects to the Bicentennial Sculpture Garden. Although there's no grassy areas on which to spread a picnic blanket, the Art Gallery's café has outdoor seating as part of the gardens.

At a glance

Address: Art Gallery Road, Campbelltown

Map ref: G 511/D7, S 368/G11, U 346/H7

Public transport: Campbelltown or Macarthur Stations (both about 1.2 km), Busways buses 891 from Campbelltown and 890 from Macarthur (both stop within 200 m)

Parking: Unrestricted in gallery car park, closes at 1600

Entry fee: None

Opening times: 1000-1600

BBQs: No

Boating: No

Dogs: No

Kiosk/café: Art Gallery café open 1000-1600, T 4645 4333

Playground: No

Power/lights: No

Shade: Trees and gazebo shelters

Swimming: No

Tables: Benches only in the gardens

Toilets: Yes

Water: At the café

Wheelchairs: Toilets, good access

111 Simmos Beach

At a glance

Address: Helicia Road, Macquarie Fields

Map refs: G 454/K6, S 330/M18, U 308/Q6

Public transport: None

Parking: Unrestricted car park, closes at sunset

Entry fee: None

Opening times: As car park

BBQs: Gas (free)

Boating: No

Dogs: Leashed, not on beach

Kiosk/café: No

Playground: No

Power/lights: No

Shade: Plenty of trees

Swimming: River

Tables: Many

Toilets: Yes

Water: Taps

Wheelchairs: Toilet, access to BBQ area, but not to the beach

This small river beach has leant its name to a large area of surrounding remnant bush, now preserved as a reserve and accessible by a number of bush tracks. The beach itself is accessed via steps from the surprisingly large main picnic and BBQ area (there is another a few hundred metres away). This is very much a bush and river experience, with no open areas. These are the upper reaches of Georges River, and depths can be very uneven so diving in is not recommended.

112 Chipping Norton Lakes

This fine regional park and wildlife refuge is located along the Georges River, where bushland, cycleways, sporting fields and a whopping nine separate picnic areas, each with different facilities, surround a series of wetlands and waterways. The picnic areas at the south-west corner are connected by a 1.6 kilometre paved walkway following the lake's foreshore, and are popular with birdwatchers, small family groups and locals fishing from the bridge at Haigh Park. The north-east corner, with its boat ramps and superior playgrounds, tends to attract bigger groups, especially on weekends.

At a glance

Address: Homestead Avenue, Chipping Norton

Map refs (Homestead): G 366/G12, S 291/M16, U 250/B12

Public transport: From Liverpool Station, Busways bus 861, or Warwick Farm Station (1.5 km)

Parking: Unrestricted car park, closes at sunset

Entry fee: None

Opening times: 0830-sunset

BBQs: Electric (free) except for Chauvel, Grand Flanneur and Riverside

Boating: Boat ramps at Angle and Grand Flanneur

Dogs: Leashed

Kiosk/café: No

Playground: There are six playgrounds, the best at Black Muscat

Power/lights: No

Shade: Trees and shelters. Large group shelters at Angle, Black Muscat, Haigh, Homestead and South

Swimming: Not recommended (although locals do)

Tables: Yes

Toilets: At Angle, Black Muscat, Haigh, Homestead and South

Water: Bubblers

Wheelchairs: Disabled toilets, access to all areas except Thomas Moore and Chauvel

113 Mirambeena Regional Park

A strip of green running along Prospect Creek, Mirambeena consists of five separate parks: Garrison Point, Lake Gillawarna, Flinders Slopes, Shortland Brush and Lansdowne Reserve. Each park has something special: great playgrounds at Garrison Point, birdwatching at Lake Gillawarna, the privately run Barnaby's Restaurant at Shortland Brush, exercise tracks at Flinders Slopes and an off-road model car track at Lansdowne Reserve. On Australia Day, there's a huge carnival at Garrison Point.

At a glance

Address: Henry Lawson Drive, Georges Hall

Map refs (Garrison Point): G 367/C13, S 292/C17, U 250/H13

Public transport: The 907 Veolia bus stops on Woodville Rd nr Allowrie Rd (1.2 km to nearest part of park)

Parking: Unrestricted car park, closes 1900

Entry fee: None

Opening times: 0800-1900

BBQs: Electric (free) and wood (wood provided) at Flinders, Garrison and Gillawarna

Boating: No

Dogs: Leashed

Kiosk/café: Barnaby's Restaurant at Shortland Brush, open Tue-Sat

Playground: At Flinders, Garrison and Gillawarna (the best is at Gillawarna)

Power/lights: No

Shade: Plenty of trees, lots of sheltered tables

Swimming: Not recommended (though people do)

Tables: Yes

Toilets: Yes

Water: Taps

Wheelchairs: Toilets and good access at Garrison and Gillawarna

Despite having a slightly neglected feel, Georges River is a significant park in this area and very popular with bushwalkers, boaters and anglers. There are two main picnic areas, the best maintained, but less peaceful, being Fitzpatrick Park. This large grassy area, adjacent to the river, has a small beach and a couple of electric BBQs. Burrawang and Cattle Duffers are further from the main road, with the latter being particularly tranquil, though with the least facilities.

At a glance

Address: Bayview Avenue, Undercliffe

Map refs Fitzpatrick G 428/C13, S 332/N9, U 291/C13

Public transport: None close

Parking: Unrestricted car parks open to 1830 (1930 daylight saving)

Entry fee: $7 per car (or NPWS pass); unrestricted street parking by the entrances to Fitzpatrick

Opening times: 24 hours

BBQs: Electric (free) in Fitzpatrick and Burrawang

Boating: Ramp inside entrance to Burrawang; private ramp (The Boatshed) outside lower entrance to Fitzpatrick ($5)

Dogs: No

Kiosk/café: Drinks and snacks from the Boatshed, outside entrance to Fitzpatrick

Playground: No

Power/lights: No

Shade: Plenty of trees, some sheltered tables

Swimming: Not recommended

Tables: Sheltered at Burrawang, couple at Fitzpatrick

Toilets: Yes

Water: Taps at toilets

Wheelchairs: Toilets at Fitzpatrick; good access

At a glance

Address: Oatley Park Avenue, Oatley

Map refs: G 430/F12, S 334/D8, U 292/L12

Public transport: Oatley Station (1.8 km), from the station Punchbowl bus 954 stops on Short St (300 m)

Parking: Unrestricted car park

Entry fee: None

Opening times: 0800-sunset

BBQs: Electric (free) and wood (wood provided)

Boating: No

Bookings: Bookings for Oatley Park Castle, T 9330 6209

Dogs: Leashed

Kiosk/café: No

Playground: At the adjacent Steamroller Park: flying fox, seesaw, swings and a much-loved old steam roller

Power/lights: No

Shade: Lots of sheltered tables, including shelter for large groups at 'The Castle'

Swimming: Yes

Tables: Yes

Toilets: Yes

Water: Bubblers, taps

Wheelchairs: Toilet, good access

The 45 hectares of Oatley Park, with three out of four boundaries defined by water, is the largest and most intact parcel of remnant bushland in the region. The picnic area is at the southern end of the park next to Oatley Baths, a popular swimming spot set in a horseshoe bay protected by year-round shark nets. The unabashed kitsch of the 'Castle', built by unemployed workers during The Depression, provides shelter for large groups.

Wanda Beach

South & Royal National Park

To the south of Botany Bay, the best picnic-spot destination is undoubtedly the Royal National Park. Established in 1879, the much-loved 'Royal' was Australia's first national park. It has a colourful history of public recreation, including the kind of things people don't normally associate with national parks, such as dance halls, huge ornamental gardens and the introduction of animals, such as rabbits and foxes for hunting.

Today, the Royal retains its diverse range of landscapes, including some of Sydney's best beaches, an extensive network of bushwalking and cycle tracks, and the wild Hacking River, ideal for canoeing and tiloing. Some of the picnic areas can get very busy, but even on peak days in midsummer it's still possible to find a quiet spot.

Outside the park, there are some accessible spots along the Georges and Woronora Rivers, a well thought-out picnic area at Woronora Dam, and the long stretches of beaches at Brighton-le-Sands and Cronulla.

Tucked a little way inland from the long string of Brighton-Le-Sands beaches, this relatively new park has benefited from more thoughtful design than that of many older small urban parks. Although the adjacent road is busy, most of the facilities are set well back. A family bike track encircles most of the large grassy area, within which are a playground, tables and BBQs. Beyond this area is a short stretch of water, fringed with trees, and beyond that a small area of bush.

At a glance

Address: West Botany Street, Rockdale

Map refs: G 433/G32, S 316/C19, U 294/M3

Public transport: Kogarah Station (1.2 km), buses 475-477 stop at Rockdale Plaza (500 m)

Parking: Unrestricted car park

Entry fee: None

Opening times: 24 hours

BBQs: Electric (free)

Boating: No

Dogs: Leashed

Kiosk/café: No

Playground: Slides, swings, climbing frames; bike paths

Power/lights: No

Shade: A few trees, sheltered tables

Swimming: No

Tables: Yes

Toilets: Yes

Water: Bubblers/taps

Wheelchairs: Good access

This large reserve is mostly grass, but has lots of trees shading much of the area. Facilities are generous and well spaced out, and you're likely to find a spare BBQ even if the reserve is fairly busy (as it frequently is). The adjacent beach — the southernmost of the Brighton-Le-Sands set — is brilliantly white and two groynes have been used to create a netted swimming area.

At a glance

Address: Russell Avenue, Dolls Point

Map refs: G 463/G2, S 336/C14, J 314/M2

Public transport: The 478 bus stops on Ramsgate Rd (1 km)

Parking: Car park unrestricted between 0500-2200

Entry fee: None

Opening times: 24 hours

BBQs: Electric (free)

Boating: No

Dogs: Leashed in reserve

Kiosk/café: Coffee in the Park, open daily 0900-1700; also Beach Hut restaurant

Playground: Large climbing rope pyramid

Power/lights: No

Shade: Many trees, one large shelter with tables

Swimming: Harbour beach with netted area, not patrolled

Tables: Yes

Toilets: Yes

Water: Taps

Wheelchairs: Good access

118 Carrs Bush Park

This large popular reserve is mostly lawn, but has a great number of trees shading much of the area. Abundant facilities are well spaced out, except for the BBQs which are all grouped together in a communal area, so you may have a fairly long stroll with the snags. The park has both a huge netted swimming area and modest beach, plus an Olympic pool complex next door.

At a glance

Address: Carwar Avenue, Carrs Park

Map refs: G 432/G16, S 335/J12, U 294/B16

Public transport: The 959, 970 and 971 Veolia buses all stop on Princes Hwy, the 958 stops on Carlton Cresent

Parking: Unrestricted car park, open 0500-2030

Entry fee: None

Opening times: 24 hours

BBQs: Electric (free) in one central area

Boating: Boat ramps just south off Princes Hwy

Dogs: Leashed

Kiosk/café: In Olympic pool area, entry payment not required

Playground: Slides, swings, climbing frames

Power/lights: No

Shade: Many trees, large shelters with multiple tables

Swimming: Netted harbour area; Olympic Pool (T 9546 5983), open 0530-2030 Mon-Fri, 0800-1700 Sat-Sun

Tables: Many

Toilets: Yes

Water: Bubblers/taps

Wheelchairs: Good access

At a glance

Address: Cape Solander Drive, Kurnell

Map refs: G 466/D6, S 337P18, U 316/J6

Public transport: None

Parking: Unrestricted car park, open 1000-1630; unrestricted on Captain Cook Street

Entry fee: $7 per car (or NPWS Pass)

Opening times: 24 hours

BBQs: Gas (free)

Boating: No

Dogs: No

Kiosk/café: Snacks and drinks from the Discovery Centre, open 1100-1500 Mon-Fri, 1000-1630 Sat-Sun

Playground: No

Power/lights: No

Shade: Many trees, most tables sheltered

Swimming: Rocky harbour beach

Tables: Yes

Toilets: Yes

Water: Bubblers/taps

Wheelchairs: Toilets, good access

Captain Cook's first point of landfall in Australia is preserved as part of Botany Bay National Park. Surrounded by bush, the actual landfall area is now a large, mainly tree-covered, grassy area. There are views right around the bay and over to Sydney Airport, so this is a great place for aircraft and ship-spotters. The BBQ areas are set well back from the shore, close to the Discovery Centre which has an interesting area presenting the history of the landfall and of the Aboriginal people that lived in this area. Several bush tracks fan out from the Discovery Centre to the south around the rest of Kurnell Peninsula.

120 Wanda Beach

Part of the long crescent of Cronulla beaches, Wanda is the most accessible area at the northern end. It's a lot less busy than the main beaches further south, and even on days when it does get a little crowded, you simply have to walk north until you find a quieter spot. Facilities are modest but include toilets, showers and a kiosk. This is a popular surfing beach and, when the wind gets up, is also a major draw for kite surfers.

At a glance

Address: Murdock Street, North Cronulla

Map refs: G 494/D7, S 356/K15, U 335/D7

Public transport: Cronulla Station (1.8 km), the 984 Crowther bus stops on Elouera Rd (800 m)

Parking: Unrestricted on local streets

Entry fee: None

Opening times: 24 hours

BBQs: No

Boating: No

Dogs: Leashed, only in indicated areas

Kiosk/café: Wanda Beach Kiosk, open daily 0800-1600 (when sufficient business)

Playground: Climbing frame

Power/lights: No

Shade: Very little

Showers: Yes

Snorkelling: No

Surfing: Yes

Swimming: Ocean, patrolled, but notorious for rips

Tables: Yes

Toilets: Yes

Water: Taps

Wheelchairs: Not good access

Just to the south of central Cronulla, Shelly Park provides an alternative to the main town beaches. The large grassy area is fringed by palms and Norfolk Island pines, providing plenty of shade, and slopes down to a small beach area and rock baths. The surrounding rock platforms and pools are usually of much interest to children, and if the seas are calm, the long rock gutter that runs all the way to Cronulla Point provides excellent snorkelling.

At a glance

Address: Ewos Parade, Cronulla

Map refs: G 494/A16, S 376/G4, J 335/A16

Public transport: Cronulla Station (1 km), the 984 Crowther bus stops at the station

Parking: Unrestricted parking on Ewos Pde

Entry fee: None

Opening times: 24 hours

BBQs: Electric (free)

Boating: No

Dogs: Leashed on paths

Kiosk/café: No

Playground: Slides, swings, climbing frames

Power/lights: No

Shade: Some trees, sheltered tables

Snorkelling: Excellent along rock gutter

Swimming: Rock baths

Tables: Yes

Toilets: Yes

Water: Taps

Wheelchairs: Good access, including to rock baths

Far beneath, and out of sight of the Menai Bridge, this quiet spot is adjacent to a popular boat ramp giving access to the Woronora River. A large grassy area is dotted with a couple of sheltered tables, BBQs and a playground, and there are a few tables in the more bushy areas a little way along the river. From the main area, walking tracks head up the steep, bush-covered valley and circle through the Burnum Burnum Sanctuary, with a couple of lookouts along the way.

At a glance

Address: Menai Road, Woronora

Map refs: G 460/G13, S 353/R5, U 312/G13

Public transport: None close

Parking: Unrestricted car park, closes 2000 (2200 daylight saving)

Entry fee: None

Opening times: 0600-2000 (2200 daylight saving)

BBQs: Electric (free)

Boating: Boat ramp

Dogs: Leashed

Kiosk/café: No

Playground: Slides, swings, climbing frames

Power/lights: Lighting

Shade: Sheltered tables

Swimming: River

Tables: Yes

Toilets: Yes

Water: Taps

Wheelchairs: Toilet, good access

123 Prince Edward Park, Woronora

Further up the Woronora River from the Jannali Reserve, and on the junction between the river and Forbes Creek, this peaceful picnic area is adjacent to a large playing field. The main attractions here are the bushwalks into the park proper (accessed across the road) and the opportunity to hire canoes or kayaks and explore further up Woronora River or Forbes Creek. You'll find quite a few other quiet waterside spots along the way.

At a glance

Address: Prince Edward Park Road, Woronora

Map refs: G 489/J2, S 353/N10, J 332/D2

Public transport: None close

Parking: Unrestricted car park

Entry fee: None

Opening times: 24 hours

BBQs: No

Boating: Kayak/canoe/motor boat hire from Star Boatshed (T 9545 584, just over the bridge from the park), from $15/hr. Open 0830-1800 daily in summer, check ahead in winter. Also a boat ramp in the car park

Dogs: Leashed

Kiosk/café: Drinks and snacks from the Star Boatshed

Playground: No

Power/lights: No

Shade: Some trees, sheltered tables

Swimming: River

Tables: Yes

Toilets: Yes

Water: No

Wheelchairs: Toilets, good access

Royal National Park

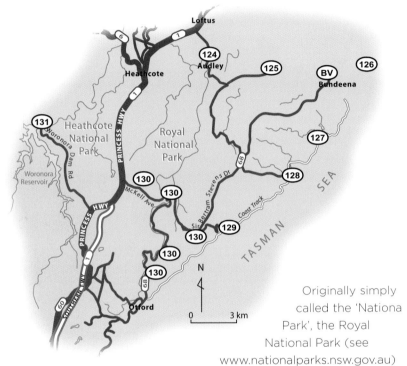

Originally simply called the 'Nationa Park', the Royal National Park (see www.nationalparks.nsw.gov.au) was declared in 1879, following the lead taken by the United States seven years earlier when they established Yellowstone, the world's first national park. The park is very extensive given its proximity to a major city, and much of it is accessible via a couple of sealed roads and the many walking tracks and fire trails.

Vegetation varies as dramatically as the landscape, with a predominance of heath on the plateau areas, varied woodland along sheltered creeklines, mangroves along the tidal reaches of the rivers and lush rainforest remnants in the Narrabeen soils to the south,

The beaches vary dramatically too, from easily accessible and extremely popular spots such as Wattamolla, to quiet and off-the-beaten track places such as Little Marley, North Era or Werrong, the nudist beach near the southern end. Wattamolla and Audley are the main picnic areas, though there are a number of smaller, simpler — and quieter — sites further south.

Camping is allowed at Bonnie Vale camping ground (near the small village of Bundeena), Providential Point, North Era and Uloola Falls. Pre-booking is required and you need to allow enough time for the NPWS to post you your permit (T 9542 0683). Also, although water is available in places, it isn't potable and needs to be treated or boiled.

Cycling and mountain biking are popular, and bikes, pedal boats, row boats and kayaks can be hired from the historic Audley Boatshed (T 9545 4967). Except during total fire bans, portable gas BBQs can be used in the park. There is a visitor centre at Audley, where you can pick up a useful map and guide for just $1. Aside from the main through roads, the park is closed from 2030-0700. For more information on the 2-day Coast Track and other walks see the park website or our companion title *Sydney's Best Bush, Park and City Walks*.

Audley is one of the most popular picnic areas in this park, attracting over 400,000 visitors every year. The sweeping lawned areas and ornamental trees were part of the Victorian 'pleasure gardens' in the 1800s and these elements remain today, with eight separate picnic areas, a simple kiosk and the historic Audley Boatshed, from where you can hire bikes, boats and kayaks. Alternatively, bring your own simple craft or a lilo, make up a gourmet hamper, and spend the day paddling the dreamy waters of the Hacking River.

At a glance

Address: Sir Bertram Stevens Drive, Royal National Park

Map refs: G 520/E5, S 374/C9, U 352/K5

Public transport: Parkline Tram from Loftus Railway Station, Wed, Sun and public holidays (plus a 1.5 km walk). T 9542 3646, or see www.sydneytramwaymuseum.com.au

Parking: Unrestricted car park, closes 2030

Entry fee: $11 vehicle fee to Royal NP or NPWS pass

Opening times: 0700-2030

BBQs: Gas (free) at Ironbark Flat and Reids Flat, wood BBQs elsewhere (wood provided)

Boating: Audley Boatshed hires out pedal boats, row boats and kayaks. Open daily, 0900-1700 (T 9545 4967)

Dogs: No

Kiosk/café: Open 7 days, 0930-1700, T 9521 2240

Playground: No

Power/lights: No

Shade: Lots of trees, some shelters

Swimming: Yes, but see opposite for details

Tables: Yes

Toilets: Yes

Water: Taps

Wheelchairs: Toilets and access and at Allambie Flat and Currawong Flat

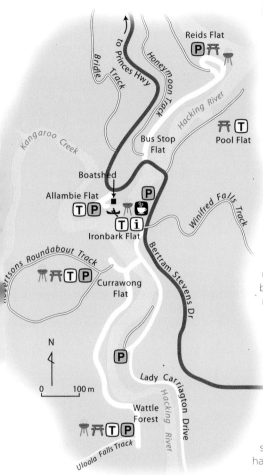

Swimming at Audley

Some people get confused about whether swimming is allowed at Audley Picnic Area or not. Swimming is fine in Kangaroo Creek (which comes in from behind the boatshed and meets up with the Hacking River), and indeed, there are some lovely waterholes worth exploring just a little upstream along this waterway. On the other hand, swimming isn't recommended in the Hacking River immediately upstream of the causeway, because the water is very reedy and people can get a sense of being 'dragged down'. (In reality, lots of people do swim here in summer, especially when fooling around on simple water craft and lilos.) Swimming is also not recommended in the salty waters downstream of the causeway, for the more sobering reason that sharks have been sighted here.

125 Warumbul Picnic Area

Definitely off the beaten track — in fact the last 2 km are via a dirt road — Warumbul is on the southern shore of Port Hacking, with views over to Lilli Pilli and east right up to the entrance of the harbour. Small grassy areas slope down to a crumbling wharf area and a small adjacent beach. Facilities are modest, and the usually remains a peaceful spot even when the rest of the park is overrun.

At a glance

Address: Warumbul Road, Royal National Park

Map refs: G 522/B6, S 375/D10, U 353/M6

Public transport: None

Parking: Unrestricted car park, access road closes 2030

Entry fee: $11 per vehicle or NPWS pass

Opening times: 0700-2030

BBQs: No

Boating: No

Dogs: No

Kiosk/café: No

Playground: No

Power/lights: No

Shade: Some trees

Swimming: Harbour beach, not patrolled

Tables: No

Toilets: Yes

Water: No

Wheelchairs: Not good access

126 Jibbon Beach

This long, flat and narrow beach, backed by bush, has gentle ripples ideal for small children and those who don't like surf. If you treasure privacy there a few pretty rocky coves around the corner, accessible from the bush track to Jibbon Head. This short coastal track is well worth taking for the views north and Aboriginal engraving site just off the path. Jibbon Beach's north-facing position is unusual in Sydney, so may be protected when the other beaches are too windy. Cronulla lies just opposite, on the far side of Port Hacking.

At a glance

Address: Neil Street, Bundeena

Map refs: G 524/C8, S 376/J12, U 355/C8

Public transport: Bundeena Ferry from Cronulla (T 9523 2990) www.cronullaferries.com.au

Parking: Unrestricted parking on Neil Street

Entry fee: None, unless coming by vehicle ($11 entry fee per vehicle or NPWS pass)

Opening times: 24 hours (from Bundeena)

BBQs: No

Boating: No

Dogs: No

Kiosk/café: Several in Bundeena, on the road uphill from ferry wharf

Playground: No

Power/lights: No

Shade: Some trees

Showers: No

Snorkelling: Yes

Surfing: Jibbon Bombora, just south of Jibbon Head

Swimming: Sheltered ocean beach, not patrolled

Tables: No

Toilets: Nearest are in Bundeena, about 50 m uphill from wharf

Water: No

Wheelchairs: Not good access

Marley Beach and its sibling to the south, Little Marley, are two of Sydney's best beaches if complete rugged isolation and natural beauty is what you seek. These beaches can only be reached by walking along the cliffs from Bundeena or Wattamolla, and there are no facilities, so they see little in the way of foot traffic. In fact, once you are on these beaches there is not a man-made object in sight. Marley is backed by deep dunes and a lagoon but the beach itself is highly dangerous for swimming. Take the one kilometre path around the rocks to reach the more sheltered Little Marley Beach for a swim.

At a glance

Address: Foot access via Coast Track from Bundeena (7 km) or Wattamolla Beach (3 km)

Map refs: See map on page 174, or refer to Royal National Park Map and Guide

Public transport: None

Parking: No nearby vehicular access

Entry fee: None, unless coming by vehicle via Wattamolla ($11 entry fee per vehicle or NPWS pass)

Opening times: Effectively 24 hours (from Bundeena) but no camping, otherwise 0700-2030

BBQs: No

Boating: No

Dogs: No

Kiosk/café: No

Playground: No

Power/lights: No

Shade: No

Showers: No

Snorkelling: No

Surfing: Yes, at Little Marley

Swimming: Not recommended at Marley due to dangerous rips

Tables: No

Toilets: No

Water: No

Wheelchairs: No access

Marley Beach

128 Wattamolla Beach and Picnic Area

The most popular destination in the Royal National Park, the beach at Wattamolla is set back in a cove making it sheltered and relatively safe for swimming. Behind the beach, a waterfall tumbles down into a picture-perfect lagoon, shaded all around with casuarinas, with ample space for picnics. At the top of the small cliffs overlooking the lagoon are two large grassy picnic areas, with excellent BBQ facilities. The Coast Track can be followed from the cove both north and south. As picnic locations go, it doesn't get much better than this.

At a glance

Address: Wattamolla Road, Royal National Park

Map refs: See map on page 174, or refer to Royal National Park Map and Guide

Public transport: None

Parking: Unrestricted car park, access road closes 2030

Entry fee: $11 per vehicle or NPWS pass

Opening times: 0700-2030

BBQs: Electric (free), portable gas BBQs permitted except during total fire bans

Boating: No

Camping: Limited bush camping at nearby Providential Point. T 9542 0683 to book. No bookings or permits available at the site itself

Dogs: No

Kiosk/café: Weekends when busy, and summer holidays

Playground: No

Power/lights: No

Shade: Plenty of trees on foreshore and in picnic areas

Showers: Yes

Snorkelling: Yes, in the lagoon

Surfing: No

Swimming: Lagoon and sheltered ocean beach (not patrolled)

Tables: Yes, mostly sheltered by trees

Toilets: Yes

Water: Taps (not drinkable)

Wheelchairs: Access to picnic areas, but not good access to beach

129 Garie Beach

This is the main surf beach in the Royal National Park, as it's also one of the most exposed as well as accessible. Steep headlands rise up at either end with access to the Coast Track which heads off both north and south. Parking is much more limited than at Wattamolla, but is allowed further up the access road. At the time of writing (early 2007) a large new Surf Safety Centre was under construction, including new Surf Lifesaving Club buildings, a first aid room, hall, kiosk, picnic area and landscaping.

At a glance

Address: Garie Road, Royal National Park

Map refs: See map on page 174, or refer to Royal National Park Map and Guide

Public transport: None

Parking: Unrestricted car park, access road closes 2030

Entry fee: $11 per vehicle or NPWS pass

Opening times: 0700-2030

BBQs: Not at time of writing, though a picnic area with BBQs is planned

Boating: No

Dogs: No

Kiosk/café: Under construction at time of writing

Playground: No

Power/lights: No

Shade: Shade at northern end in the afternoons

Showers: Under construction at time of writing

Snorkelling: No

Surfing: Yes, powerful beach breaks

Swimming: Ocean, patrolled

Tables: Not at time of writing, though a picnic area with tables is planned

Toilets: Yes

Water: No

Wheelchairs: Toilets; not good access

There are a number of other picnic spots in the park, all simple grassy enclaves in the inland forested areas to the south. Although there are no facilities at any of these locations, the upside is they're not so popular, and even on a busy day you're likely to have the place to yourself. Those accessible by road include: Gunjulla Flat and Waterfall Flat on McKell Avenue; Red Cedar Flat and Karingal on the banks of the Hacking River (a shaded bushwalk winds through remnant rainforest, linking these two areas), and Upper Causeway on the banks of Waterfall Creek.

At a glance

Address: Southern Royal National Park

Map refs: See map on page 174, or refer to Royal National Park Map and Guide

Public transport: None

Parking: Unrestricted car parks

Entry fee: $11 per vehicle or NPWS pass

Opening times: 0700-2030

BBQs: Wood BBQs in some places, portable gas stoves permitted except during fire bans

Boating: No

Dogs: No

Kiosk/café: No

Playground: No

Power/lights: No

Shade: Many trees

Swimming: No, but children love to paddle in the shallow waters next to many of these areas

Tables: No

Toilets: No

Water: No

Wheelchairs: Generally good access

Little known and a fair drive from Sydney, this picnic area can still get quite busy on those perfect summer Sundays, but always remains a peaceful spot. You're able to walk right across the dam, and the views over the dam, reservoir and spillway certainly grab attention. There are several picnic areas. The upper areas are well-shaded, with several large grassy areas. Facilities are very good with large shelters accommodating several tables and BBQs.

At a glance

Address: Woronora Dam Road, near Waterfall

Map ref: See map on page 174

Public transport: None

Parking: Unrestricted car park, closed 1700 (1900 weekends during daylight saving)

Entry fee: None

Opening times: 1000-1700 (1900 weekends during daylight saving)

BBQs: Electric (free)

Boating: No

Dogs: Leashed

Kiosk/café: No

Playground: Slides, swings, climbing frames

Power/lights: No

Shade: Many trees, sheltered tables

Swimming: No

Tables: Many

Toilets: Yes

Water: Bubblers/taps

Wheelchairs: Toilets, good access

Safety tips

Sun

Australians have this advice drummed into them from birth but visitors should be aware that Australian sun is very strong and you will get burnt in as little as ten minutes if you don't take precautions. Always wear sunscreen, a hat and have a long-sleeved shirt handy if you'll be out in the sun for a prolonged period.

Swimming

When swimming on a beach patrolled by life guards, always swim between the flags. If the beach is not patrolled look out for signs indicating rip areas, and ask locals if at all unsure. A rip is a strong current running out to sea and is indicated by dark or murky water, a rippled surface or water than generally looks different to that around it.

 See the Surf Life Saving Australia website, www.slsa.asn.au, for more information. Sydney has many rock pools by the beach so if you are not confident in the sea or surf, it may be best to swim in one of these pools.

Bites and bluebottles

At certain times of year, lots of bluebottles wash up on some Sydney beaches. If you get stung by a 'bluey', the official SLSA treatment is to remove all stingers, wash off in fresh water as soon as possible, and then apply an ice pack or ice to the affected area.

On the other hand, some folk swear by vinegar as being effective in relieving pain, while others say that holding the sting under water that's as hot as you can bear for at least 15 minutes does the trick. Whatever you do, don't rub sand into the bite as this just spreads the venom deeper into your skin. Also, seek medical help if the pain continues.

If wading around in shallow water over a reef, wear a pair of old sneakers or waterproof sandals to protect you from treading on something venomous or from cutting your feet.

Sharks

There hasn't been a fatal shark attack in Sydney since 1963 and only ten non-fatal shark attacks in the last forty years. Part of the reason for such low fatalities is that most of the surf beaches are protected

by meshing, a net slung close to the ocean floor to entangle sharks, and most popular harbour beaches are protected by rigid shark enclosures. In reality, the risk of an attack is infinitesimal and millions of people have swum safely at Sydney's beaches. However, if you're swimming at a beach that doesn't have nets, you're best to avoid river mouths or drop-offs to deep water, and avoid swimming at dusk or at night. If you still feel afraid to go in, swim in a rock pool or netted harbour beach.

Snakes

It is very unlikely you that will encounter a snake on any of these walks but Sydney does have four species of venomous snakes; the Red-bellied Black snake, the Eastern Tiger, Eastern Brown and the Brown Tree Snake. Most snakes are more afraid of you than you are of them, and will only bite if trodden on, cornered or harassed. Avoid striding through long grass and try to keep to tracks. If the path is obscured, make plenty of noise as you walk. If you do see a snake, give it a wide berth.

If you do get bitten by a snake stay calm. Place a folded pad over the bite and then apply a firm bandage over the pad and as far up the limb towards the heart as you can. Remain as still as possible and keep the limb immobile using a splint if available. Do not walk but send somebody else for help or wait for a passer-by. Do not cut, suck or wash the bite and do not apply a tourniquet. Seek urgent medical attention. A description of the snake, and residual venom on your skin, will help with swift identification and treatment. Anti-venom is available for most snake bites.

Surfing in Sydney

Surfers travel from all around the world to visit Sydney's surf beaches, enjoying amazing waves, glorious scenery and Australia's laid-back beach culture.

Throughout Sydney there are some great waves, but the further you get from the city centre, the less crowded the beaches are. The quietest time is early morning when the sun is rising or during late autumn and winter, when you may find it's just you, the rolling surf and the dolphins. In contrast, the city beaches such as Manly or Bondi — especially during summer — can get very crowded, with a party vibe that runs from dawn to dusk.

Beach	Page	Hazard rating	Best conditions
Bilgola	99	6	NE-S swell, W wind
Bondi	34	7	SE swell, NW wind
Bronte	37	7	E-SE swell, SW-NW wind
Bungan	98	7	NE-E swell, W-SW wind
Collaroy	94	5	Large E-SE swell, W-SW wind
Coogee	38	4	A big swell and NW-SW wind
Dee Why	92	6	Big swells off southern rock platform with S-SW wind (experienced surfers only)
Freshwater	90	7	East swell, NE-W wind, mid-high tide
Garie	182	7	E-NE swell, W-N wind
Manly	88	6	E-SE swell, W wind
Maroubra	40	6	E-NE swell, N-SW wind
Mona Vale	97	7	NE-E swell for point break on northern reef
North Steyne	88	6	Big swells following high seas (experienced surfers onl
Palm	102	6	SW-NW wind for beach breaks, NE-NW for Barrenjoey
Tamarama	36	8	Breaks on northern reef during northerly swells (experienced surfers only)
Turimetta	96	7	NE-S swell, NE wind
Whale	101	6	NE-S swell, NW wind

Best surfing conditions

The best time of day for surfing is usually first thing in the morning, before the northeasterly wind gets up (Sydney's prevailing wind in summer). Once the northeasterly gets going, you'll need to hunt out more protected spots, such as the northern corners of more southerly-facing beaches.

You'll soon get an instinct about what happens where. When seas are relatively calm, the more open (longer) beaches pick up more swell. Although the table below has comments about the best swell and wind conditions for each beach in this book, what works best for you depends on your skill and experience, and what kind of conditions you enjoy best. For updates on daily surf conditions, visit **www.swellnet. com.au**, **www.coastalwatch.com.au** and **www.realsurf.com.au**.

Comments
Good beach breaks for beginners during small swells, but treacherous rip at southern end in bigger conditions
Beginners should head for North Bondi
Dangerous rips, steep sandbanks
Left-hander at northern end, beach breaks
Good for beginners during small swells
Not really a surf beach, small reef at southern end only
Beach breaks or southern corner during small swells good for beginners
Great break during summer north-easters
Left-hander at northern end, powerful beach breaks
Good beginners beach in calm conditions
Consistent beach breaks in most conditions
At southern end, break known to locals as Cooks Terrace
Fairy Bower is one of the most famous point breaks in Sydney
Great beach breaks, left-hander at northern end (Barrenjoey Point)
Closed to board riders during patrol hours
Strong shore break, good at northern end
Beach breaks, plus the Wedge at the northern end is a famous break during big NE swells (experienced surfers only)

Surfing in Sydney

Getting started & surfing safely

Don't go surfing unless you're a confident swimmer who is used to waves and being in the surf. If you're not, spend some time mucking around in the water for a few days to get acclimatised, and maybe try boogie-boarding first.

Lots of fun can be had, but you won't learn how to surf overnight. You'll probably want to start by practicing on the broken waves coming into shore, and only after mastering the whitewater — which may take many sessions to achieve — attempt to start catching unbroken waves. A slow peeling point break is a predictable wave and is the ideal way to begin. Use a board that's either long or stable, or both.

The most important thing is to respect the waves. Don't go out in conditions you can't handle, and don't stay out for so long that you get completely exhausted. Always be confident that you have enough energy and skill to swim back to shore if your leg-rope should break. If you find yourself getting thrown about and you feel you're not coping, don't push yourself. Try again another day or go to another spot.

Surf Schools

Name & Suburb	Phone	Web
Cronulla Surf School Cronulla	9544 0433	www.cronullasurf.com.au
Lets go Surfing North Bondi	9365 1800	www.letsgosurfing.com.au
Manly Surf School Manly and Palm Beach	9977 6977	www.manlysurfschool.com
Sydney North Surf School Narrabeen	0415 211 955	www.sydneynorthsurfschool.com.au
Sydney Safe Surf Schools Maroubra	9365 4370	www.safesurfschools.com.au
Sydney Surf Experience In and around Sydney	1800 888 732	www.sydneysurf.com.au
Surf Lifesaving Australia All around Sydney	9300 4000	www.slsa.com.au
Waves Surf School Coogee, Bondi	1800 851 101	www.wavessurfschool.com.au

Surfing in Sydney

Surf schools are a great way to get started, and most schools run half and whole day courses all year round. Alternatively, a good way to build confidence in the surf is to join your local Surf Lifesaving Club. These clubs also run 'nipper' programs designed especially for 7-13 year olds.

Useful addresses and contacts

- The **National Parks and Wildlife Service** is the governing body for all the national parks in the Sydney region. If you anticipate visiting a number of parks — or the same one on a regular basis — consider buying an annual parks pass (currently $65 per vehicle). The service also runs a series of walks and tours, some of these to places otherwise inaccessible to the general public. For more information: **www.npws.nsw.gov.au**, **T 4787 8877**.

- The **National Parks Association of NSW** has the largest activities program of its kind in Australia, including an offering of around 800 walks per year, led by over 200 experienced volunteer walks leaders. See **www.npansw.org.au**, **T 9299 0000**.

- The **Confederation of Bushwalking Clubs NSW** represents the interests of several member bushwalking clubs. Visit **www.bushwalking.org.au** to follow links to find over 20 bushwalking clubs based throughout Sydney.

- The **Historic Houses Trust** is an autonomous government authority within the Department of Arts Sports and Recreation, charged with the care of many historic buildings in New South Wales, the majority of which are in the Sydney region. The trust was initially established to run Vaucluse House and Elizabeth Bay House and now manages 14 properties. For more information on these properties and activities run by the HHT see **www.hht.net.au**.

- With not dissimilar aims to the HHT, the non-government **National Trust (NSW)** is an independent charity, founded in 1946. The Trust's role is to 'safeguard our natural, built and cultural heritage and to encourage Australians to appreciate that each generation has a responsibility to preserve our Nation's heritage for the next generation'. For more info see **www.nsw.nationaltrust.org.au**.

The 'Perfect Picnic' checklist

You certainly wouldn't want to pack everything on this suggested list every time you popped out for a sandwich in your local park, but a quick double-check before you head off on a larger scale expedition can often make a great day into a perfect day. Here are a few things you might find useful:

- Wood, firelighters and matches if you're planning on using a wood BBQ
- Sufficient gas if you're taking a gas BBQ
- A bottle opener as well as required crockery and cutlery
- Broad based cups or glasses that will stand up on uneven ground
- Cutting board and sharp knife if you're doing any food preparation
- BBQ utensils
- Condiments and accompaniments
- Ice for the Esky
- Cushions as well as a picnic rug
- Spare warm clothing in case the temperature takes a dive, and definitely a change of clothes for children if you're going to be near water (unless you're bringing swimmers)!
- Lots of drinks and lots of snacks (for extended picnics, if you keep food colouring and sugar down to a minimum the kids will last longer and do less 'crash-and-burn', but that's maybe a personal decision!)
- SPF 30 sunscreen (the higher SPF is particularly important for younger children and babies) and hats
- A packet of band-aids (their placebo effect on children is wonderful, even if the graze is so small it's invisible) and bite ointment
- Insect repellent
- A beach tent or shade umbrella you can pop the baby or young children under when they fall asleep. If you're picnicking in the bush, you might even want to take a mozzie net which you can hang from a tree to protect a sleeping child.
- A packet of 'Wet-Ones' if there's no water at the picnic spot, and a roll of toilet paper
- Plenty of change for parking meters and/or BBQs
- A generous length of rope and a water bowl if you're taking your dog
- Things that can act as weights to hold down tablecloths or picnic rugs in breezy weather
- A ball, cricket set, frisbee, boules, etc
- Camera and/or video camera
- A street directory if you're unsure of the route there
- A contingency plan if the picnic spot (or car park) turns out to be closed or too busy!
- Bags for rubbish
- A torch if you might still be out after dark

Index

A

Abbotsford, 52
Akuna Bay, 115
Andrew (Boy) Charlton Pool, 19
Apple Tree Bay, 117
Arndell, Thomas, 126
Art Gallery of NSW, 19
Ashbury, 48
Ashton Park, 72
Auburn Botanic Gardens, 146
Audley Picnic Area, 176
Avalon, 99

B

Badangi Reserve, 66
Balgowlah, 86
Balls Head, 67
Balmoral, 79-78
Balmoral Beach, 76-77
Bangalley Head, 100
Bantry Bay, 82
Bare Island Fort, 43
Barnum Barnum Sanctuary, 172
Barrenjoey Beach, 102
Barrenjoey Lighthouse, 103
Basin, The, 114
Bathers Pavilion, 77
Baulkham Hills, 137, 140
Bayview Park, 53
Beach volleyball, 89
Bents Basin, 154
Berowra Waters, 120
Berry Island, 66
Bicentennial Park, Glebe, 50
Bicentennial Park, Homebush, 56-57
Bicentennial Park, Rockdale , 166

Bidjigal Reserve, 140
Bilgola, 99, 105
Bilgola Beach, 99
Billarong Sanctuary, 95
Blaxlands Crossing Reserve, 153
Blue Mountains NP, 149-151
bluebottles, 186
Blues Point, 70
Bobbin Head, 117
Bondi Beach, 34-35
Bondi Junction, 32
Botany, 41
Botany Bay NP, 169
Bradfield Park, 68
Bradleys Head, 72
Brighton-le-Sands, 166-167
Bronte Beach, 37
Bronte Park, 37
Buffalo Creek Reserve, 62
Bundeena, 179
Bungan Beach, 98
Burrawang, 162

C

Cabarita, 54-55
Cabarita Park, 55
Callan Park, 51
Camaraigal clan, 61, 66
Camp Cove, 28
Campbelltown, 158
Canada Bay, 53
Captain Cook's Landing Place, 169
Carrs Bush Park, 168
Carrs Park, 168
Castle Hill Heritage Park, 138
Cattai NP, 126-127
Cattle Duffers, 162
Centennial Park, 30

Central Gardens, 147
Chatswood, 60
Chinamans Beach, 78
Chipping Norton Lakes, 160
Church Point, 107, 111
Clareville Beach, 104
Clark Island, 20
Clarkes Point Reserve, 63
Clifton Gardens , 75
Clontarf Reserve , 81
Coast Track, 180-182
Colebee Centre, 136
Collaroy, 93-94
Collaroy Beach, 94
Congwong Bay Beach, 44
Coogee Beach, 38
Cooks River, 46-47
Cooper Park, 32
Cremorne Point Reserve, 71
Crestwood Reserve, 137
Cronulla, 170-171
Crosslands Reserve, 121
Cumberland State Forest, 139

D

Davidson Park , 80
Dee Why Beach, 92
Dolls Point, 167
Doonside, 136
Doyles, 27

E

Edwards Beach, 76-77
Ermington, 58
Ettamogah Pub, 129
Euroka, 149
Ewen Park , 47
Exile Bay, 54

Index

F

Fagan Park, 122-123
Fagan, Bruce, 123
Fairlight Beach, 86
Farm Cove, 16
Fishermans Beach, 93
Fitzpatrick Park, 162
Flinders Slopes, 161
Florence Park, 105
Forestry Commission
    (NSW), 139
Forty Baskets Beach, 86
Frenchmans Bay, 42
Freshwater Beach, 90

G

Galston, 122-124
Galston Recreation
    Reserve, 124
Gap, The, 27
Garie Beach, 182
Garigal NP, 80, 82
Garrison Point, 161
George Kendall Riverside
    Reserve, 58
Georges Hall, 161
Georges River, 160-163
Georges River National
    Park, 162
Glebe, 50
Glenbrook, 149-151
Gough Whitlam Park, 46
Government House, 18
Governor Phillip Park, 130
Grant Reserve, 39
Great North Walk, 62
Greendale, 154
Grose Wold, 131
Gunjulla Flat, 183
Guringai tribe, 61

H

Harbord, 90
Harold Reid Reserve, 79
Harrington Park, 155
Hawkesbury River, 125
Henry Lawson Park, 52
Hermitage Foreshore Walk,
    23
Historic Houses Trust, 19,
    25, 129
HMAS Sydney, 73
HMAS Watson, 29
Home & Away, 102
Homebush, 56
Hornsby Heights, 121
Hunters Hill, 62
Hurlstone Park, 47
Hyde Park Barracks, 19

I

Icebergs, The, 35
Illawong Bay, 115

J

Jamieson Park, 95
Jamisontown, 134
Jannali Reserve, 172
Japanese Gardens, 158
Jibbon Beach, 179
Jubilee Park, 50

K

Karingal, 183
Kayak/canoe hire, 22, 63,
    76, 120, 173, 175-176
Kirribilli, 68-69
Kukundi Wildlife Shelter,
    60
Ku-Ring-Gai NP, 108-117
Kurnell, 169

L

La Perouse, 42-43
La Perouse Museum, 43
Lake Gillawarna, 161
Lake Parramatta, 141
Lane Cove NP, 60-61
Lansdowne Reserve, 161
Lawson, Henry, 52
Leichhardt Park, 51
Lilyfield, 51
Lime Kiln Head, 163
Little Congwong Bay, 44
Little Marley Beach, 180
Long Reef, 93
Luna Park, 69
Lyne Park, 22

M

Macquarie Fields, 159
Macquarie Princess, 120
Manly, 83, 87-89
Manly Beach, 88
Manly Dam, 83
Marley Beaches, 180
Maroubra Beach, 40
Martins Lookout, 133
McCallum Pool, 71
McCarrs Creek, 111
McIver Baths, 39
McMahons Point, 70
Meadowbank Memorial
    Park, 59
Mean Fiddler, 129
Merrylands West, 147
Middle Cove, 79
Middle Creek Reserve, 95
Middle Head, 74
Mirambeena Regional
    Park, 161
Mitchell Park, 127
Mona Vale, 97, 106
Mona Vale Beach, 97

Index

Mona Vale Headland, 97

Mosman, 72-75

Mount Annan Botanic Gardens, 156-157

Mountain bike circuit, 83

Mrs Macquaries Chair, 17

Mrs Macquaries Point, 17

Mulgoa, 152

N

Narrabeen Lakes, 95

National Trust (NSW), 143

Navua Reserve, 131

Nepean Belle, 134

Nepean River, 134, 153-154

Netherby Homestead, 123

Newport, 98

Nielsen Park, 24

North Harbour Reserve, 86

North Steyne Beach, 88

North Sydney Olympic Pool, 69

NSW State Library, 18

Nurraginy Reserve, 136

O

Oatley Park, 163

Oceanworld, 89

Old Government House, 143

P

Palm Beach, 102

Parkes, Sir Henry, 30-31

Parramatta, 141-143

Parramatta Park, 142

Parsley Bay Reserve, 26

Peace Park, 48

Penrith Lakes, 135

Peter Depena Reserve, 167

Pimelea Picnic Area, 148

Prince Edward Park, Cabarita, 54

Prince Edward Park, Woronora, 173

Pylon Lookout, 69

Pyrmont Point Park, 49

R

Red Cedar Flat, 183

Resolute Beach, 113

Resolute Picnic Area, 112

Robertson Park, 27

Robertsons Point, 71

Rock Lookout, 152

Rockdale, 166

Rose Bay, 22

Rosherville Reserve, 78

Rouse Hill Estate, 129

Rouse Hill Regional Park, 128

Royal Botanic Gardens , 16

Royal NP, 174-183

S

Safety, 186

Sail boat hire, 76

Scenic flights, 22, 103

Scotland Island, 107

Seaforth, 82

Sharks, 187

Shark Beach, 24

Shark Island, 21

Shelly Beach, Cronulla, 171

Shelly Beach, Manly, 87

Shelly Park, 171

Shortland Brush, 161

Simmos Beach, 159

Sir Joseph Banks Park, 41

snake bites, 187

South Head, 29

Spit-to-Manly Walk, 81, 86

Springwood, 133

Station Beach, 102

Strickland House, 23

surfing, 188-191

swimming safely, 186

Sydney Harbour Bridge, 17, 68

Sydney Harbour NP, 20-21, 29, 74

Sydney International Regatta Centre, 135

Sydney Olympic Park, 56-57

Sydney Opera House, 18

T

Tamarama Beach, 36

Taronga Zoo, 73

Tench Reserve, 134

Turimetta Beach, 96

U

Undercliffe, 46, 162

Upper Causeway, 183

V

Vaucluse, 23-26

Vaucluse House, 25

Vaucluse Park, 25

W

walking: Eastern Suburbs, 32

walking: Northern Beaches, 91

Wallacia, 152-154

Wanda Beach, 170

Warriewood, 96

Warumbul Picnic Area, 178

Waterfall Flat, 183
Watsons Bay, 27-29
Wattamolla Beach, 181
Waverton, 67
Wentworth, William
Charles, 25
West Head, 112
West Pennant Hills, 139
West Ryde, 59
Western Sydney Regional
Park, 148

Whale Beach, 101
Wheeler Park, 95
Whitlam, Gough, 46
Wildflower Gardens, 116
Windsor, 130
Winmalee, 132
Winnererremy Bay
Foreshore Reserve, 106
Wisemans Ferry Park, 125
Wollomi Pine, 157
Wollstonecraft, 66

Woolwich, 63
Woronora, 172-173
Woronora Dam, 184

Y

Yarra Bay, 42
Yellow Rock Lookout, 132

Woodslane

Woodslane are one of Australia's leading book distributors and publishers, and are delighted to be publishing this new series of *Sydney Morning Herald* outdoor guides. To browse through all the *Sydney Morning Herald*, and other titles available from Woodslane see **www.woodslane.com.au**. If your local bookshop does not have stock of one of our books they can easily order it from us for you. In case of difficulty please contact our customer service team on **+61 (0)2 9970 5111** or **info@woodslane.com.au**.

Woodslane Press books are available for bulk and custom purposes. Volume copies of this and our other titles are available at wholesale prices, and custom-jacketed and even mini-extracts are possible. Contact our Publishing Manager for further information, on **+61 (0)2 9970 5111** or **info@woodslane.com.au**.

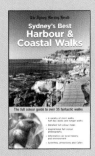

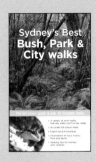

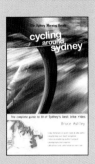

See over for more information on these great new titles.

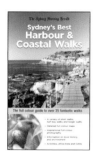

Sydney's Best Harbour & Coastal Walks

From Barrenjoey Head to the Royal National Park, Hen & Chicken Bay to North and South Heads, local author Katrina O'Brien takes us on an enriching tour of over 35 of the very best walks to be experienced along the shores of Sydney's harbour and coast. Like all our guides, the book includes full colour photography and maps, easy-to-follow instructions and great local information. Sydney's Best Harbour & Coastal Walks will be a treasured companion.

Available now • $29.99 • ISBN-13: 9781875889808

Sydney's Best Bush, Park & City Walks

After sharing the delights of the Blue Mountains best bushwalks, author Veechi Stuart turns her attention to the wealth of bush, park & city walks to be found in and around Sydney. With all the major local National Parks included and many otherwise rarely visited tracks given a new lease of life, Sydney's Best Bush, Park & City Walks will enthuse even the most experienced walkers. Sydney's Best Bush, Park & City Walks completes this series of walking guides to the near-Sydney region.

Available September 2007 • $29.95 • ISBN-13: 9781921203145

Blue Mountains Best Bushwalks

The Blue Mountains start right on the doorstep of the city of Sydney. Regardless of your fitness level or experience, the best way to discover these rugged escarpments, heart-stopping views and diverse environments is to set off on foot. Veechi Stuart, local author and resident of 20 years, combines her professional writing skills with her passion for bushwalking in her choice of the best bushwalks.

Available now • $29.99 • ISBN-13: 9781875889921

Cycling Around Sydney (4th edition)

This ride guide gives you the inspiration and confidence to get out onto quiet streets, roads and bike paths and see what Sydney and it hinterland has to offer. You'll be coasting along at a pace that lets you take it all in, your senses reeling with the sounds and smells of the bustling city and the ever-changing bush! This new, completely revised edition of Cycling Around Sydney covers a selection of 30 fantastic rides.

Available now • $24.95 • ISBN-13: 9781921203213

The Sydney Morning Herald

Photography

Many of the photographs in this book were taken by the authors, Andrew Swaffer, Veechi Stuart and Katrina O'Brien. Other photography has been supplied by Darroch Donald, Rebecca Robinson, Des Harris, Scott Townsend, John Stuart, Star Boatshed, Audely Boatshed and Jessica Baker plus a small number are courtesy of Tourism New South Wales, Mt Annan Botanic Gardens, Liverpool City Council and Historic Houses Trust of NSW.

MAP SYMBOLS & LEGEND

(i)	Tourist Information		■	Point of Interest
(T)	Toilet		+	Hospital
(P)	Car Park		╪	Place of Worship
☕	Cafe		▮	Castle
🚌	Bus Stop	△ ○		Summit, Roundabout
✋	Aboriginal Site			Marina / Wharf / Jetty
🎨	Public Art	◯		Lake / Reservoir
🐠	Aquarium	〰		Creek
🐘	Zoo	▦▦▦		Footbridge
🛒	Market			Steps / Path
❶	Place of Interest	▥▥▥▥		Bridge
H	Hotel	————		Walking Track
🤿	Snorkeling / Diving	━━━━		Walking Track / Variation
🏄	Surfing	- - - - - -		Ferry Service
🛹	Skateboarding	⬡⬡⬡⬡		Rocky Shoreline
🚴	Shared Path	++━●━++		Railway Line, Station
🦭	Swimming Pool / Rock Baths	- ○ -		Railway Station (Underground)
🏊	Swimming Enclosure	▭①▭		Freeway / Motorway
⛱	Beach	━⑩━		Highway
🐋	Whale Watching	━━━━		Major Road
⛴	Ferry Terminal	————		Minor Road
⛵	Sailing Club	━━━━		Minor Road (Unsealed)
🚣	Rowing Club	- - - - -		4WD Road / Dirt Track
🛶	Canoe Rentals	▭		Parkland / Reserve
🚲	Bicycle Path	▭		Residential / Other
⛳	Golf Course	▭		Beach / Sand Dunes
🎑	Picnic Area	▭		Ocean
🔥	BBQ	▭		Aquatic Reserve
🎠	Childrens Playground	N		
🗼	Lighthouse	⤒		
●	Start / Finish of Walk	0 200 m		
≪	View Point / Lookout			Scale

Notes

Your thoughts appreciated!

We do hope that you are enjoying using this book, but we know that nothing in this world is perfect and your suggestions for improving on this edition would be much appreciated.

Plus! Everyone who sends us useful information will go into a draw to win a picnic set (hamper, Esky, rug and various useful extras). We must receive suggestions by the end of June 2008.

Your name _____

Your address or email address _____

_____

_____

Your contact phone number _____

Are you a resident or visitor to Sydney? _____

What you most liked about this book _____

_____

_____

What you least liked about this book _____

_____

_____

Which is your favourite picnic spot featured in this book?

_____

Which is your favourite beach featured in this book?

_____

Which beach or picnic spot wasn't featured but you think should have been included?

_____

Would you like us to keep you informed of other Woodslane books?

If so: are you interested in:

☐ picnicking   ☐ general outdoor activities

☐ visiting natural & historic sites   ☐ activities in Sydney only

☐ walking   ☐ activities in NSW

☐ cycling   ☐ activities around Australia

What others books would you like to see in this series?

_____

_____

Woodslane Pty Ltd • 7/5 Vuko Place • Warriewood • NSW 2102
Fax: 02 9970 5002 • Email: picnics@woodslane.com.au